洞月亮

CAVE MOON PRESS
YAKIMA中WASHINGTON

2019

Confessions of a Hobo's Daughter

Katie Nolan

洞月亮

CAVE MOON PRESS

YAKIMA 中 WASHINGTON

ISBN: 978-0-9797785-2-0

Confessions of a Hobo's Daughter

It is true that my father was a fugitive from a chain gang. The characters, Monte and Harry, the peonage camp rescue, and the Union Square March participation are fictionalized. However, the peonage camp and Union Square March are true to history; it is just uncertain whether my father participated in these events. Other names, characters, and some events, while true, have been made composites or changed to protect privacy.

The number of people with personal memory of the Great Depression is fast shrinking with the years, and to most of us the Depression is conveyed by grainy, black-and-white images of men in hats and long coats standing in bread lines. However, although the Depression was long ago...its influence is still very much with us. In particular, the experience of the Depression helped forge a consensus that the government bears the important responsibility of...assisting people affected by economic downturns. Dozens of our most important government agencies and programs, ranging from social security (to assist the elderly and disabled) to federal deposit insurance (to eliminate banking panics) to the Securities and Exchange Commission (to regulate financial activities) were created in the 1930s, each a legacy of the Great Depression. (Remarks by Governor Ben S. Bernanke at the Parker Willis Lecture in Economic Policy, Washington and Lee University, Lexington, Virginia, March 2, 2004.)

The core of everything is love, including politics. What failure in love was exhibited during the Great Depression, when care for others was replaced with greed! What failure in love is currently being exposed by the Great Recession, when again, care for others is pushed aside for vast accumulation of wealth in the hands of a few. If we think love has nothing to do with politics, we are deluded. (Author Note)

The following are common features of people who are not living their love stories: They feel numb and traumatized.

They feel valued for what they do, not for who they are. They live on distorted beliefs.

They have failed at love and are too tired to try again.

From *The Path to Love*, Deepak Chopra

Table of Contents

Part One

Bird of Passage

1 Lay the Flattering Unction to One's Soul

Phrase meaning gladden, temper the wind to the shorn lamb, disburden: 834, Roget's Thesaurus, 1947.

The first Nolan commandment, Thou shalt turn the earth.

Katie Nolan, Green Mountain. On a spring day in 1960 my hobo father told me his terrible secret. Twenty years later, when Mt. St. Helens blew, I still kept his secret, as a mostly buried and remote memory, although sometimes I thought I would explode from the keeping of it. At the same time, the day of the revelation seemed perfectly ordinary. White clouds floated above and left shadows dancing across the landscape. A field was ploughed, all up and down until it had rough rows of dark turned earth, like giant misshapen sausages laid in parallel lines from fence to fence.

Once the earth was turned, Bud Nolan, my father, hooked the harrowing machine onto the back of the tractor and made even swirls around the field, smoothing it for grass seed. To the south, less than a mile away, looking toward Mt. St. Helens, rock bluffs peeked through the forest cover, a stony witness to the scene below. The forty acre field lay just below the snow line on the west side of the Cascade Mountains and sported rich soil from volcanic ash.

Home in the afternoon from a school event, I began to help my father. We crisscrossed the field, hand-cranking the box that held the grass seed. I walked the lower part of the forty, where it was somewhat flat, while Dad walked lightly across the wide rolling hill above, grinding out the seed.

We finished near the bridge, one plank long since missing so you could see the two feet below to Sulphur Creek. I sat dangling my feet off the edge of the bridge, and looked down between the cracks. When I glanced up, I noticed my father standing nearby, gazing across the field, motionless. I got up and stood beside him, also silent. It was then that I began to feel something for the land. It was the memory of the expression on my father's face that stayed with me, a face that was filled with the light of contentment, the kind of relaxed satisfaction one enters into after a job well done, or an artist feels after finishing a painting, then standing back to observe it. This ploughed and harrowed pasture had become Dad's perfected work of art, his Van Gogh "Sunflowers." And the earth too had light coming off of it, as it shown in the early dusk, catching the occasional drifting shadows from white clouds floating overhead. From then on, I was moved by the smell of turned earth and the lighting just before the sun went down.

We turned toward the house and strolled up the hill, past the root cellar, where Nattie Nolan, my mother, had put up jars and jars of peaches, pears, green beans, plums, and canned salmon. When I glanced over at the county road, I caught a glimpse of a black vehicle. I looked up at Dad and saw his frown. When he noticed my response to his rapid change in demeanor, he looked down at me and tried to make light of it.

"S'pose that's the FBI?" Dad said. He grinned but I thought I saw something else cross his face, an expression I couldn't understand.

He continued: "Probably just the neighbor polished his old black car. That shine won't last long on this dusty road. But never know when they might be comin' for me." Then he laughed his characteristic laugh, a chuckle tinged with irony.

"Oh, Dad..." I was about to joke back, something pithy, like ha, the FBI would likely get lost on the way. Or, that why we live out here in the middle of nowhere? But I didn't get my joke out before he spoke again.

"Yup," he said, "I've been in prison." It was in a tone of voice that I'd never heard before.

4

"I was on a chain gang and escaped," he said. He'd spoken to me as an equal, not as a fifteen-year-old daughter. What he said seemed surreal. I was jolted, thinking about prison and Dad in the same sentence. What came out was, "How did that happen?"

"Well, before I say, remember, don't tell no one 'til I'm dead. You can't trust no one, so you gotta keep it close to the chest. Even Nat don't know."

"How come you didn't tell Mom?"

"Didn't think she'd understand."

"Where did it happen?"

"Alabammy or Georgia, or somewheres."

2 It Needs No Ghost to Tell Us

Latency, also, you can see it with half an eye, the meaning lies
on the surface, thereby hangs a tale: 526,
Roget's Thesaurus, 1947.

*...CNN news inform[s] us that they had reinstituted chain gangs in the late
1990's...*

It's no wonder that truth is stranger than fiction. Fiction has to make sense.
—*Mark Twain*

Second Nolan Commandment: Thou shalt keep it close to your chest.

1930, Bud, Alabama or Georgia. As the guard crouched in front of the cage,
fumbling with the key, I nodded to Harry. Harry wrapped his arm around
the guard's throat. In one motion, I grabbed the key and unlocked the cage.
Fear flashed in the eyes of the other men. This would get them all killed—or
all free.

The guard wore a gold cross, probably a gift from the wife, under his
white T-shirt with a sweat-stained collar. He had to crouch down slightly and
bend his head to lock the cage for the night. The height of the lock was what
set him up. The cage was about the size of a circus-animal transport cage, and
looked similar, with its iron bars and metal padlock and chain.

I slipped the iron bar out of its slots. Edged the door past the guard.
Landed the bar on the side of the guard's head. I felt an eternity of nausea
when I heard the thud, the crushing of bone. I swayed as both knees buckled.
I had the urge to vomit as the bar met the skull and I heard the bone splinter.
My hands shook, and I dropped the bar next to the guard.

Then I froze, barely able to breathe. What if I killed the guy? That is something no man can retrieve. The sound of the skull cracking had the crushing weight of permanence, as if my own skull had been smashed. How could I ever return to my old self? Be fully human again?

Harry shouted. "Let's go!"

Harry was rapidly pulling the chains off the other men. I heard Harry but my eyes were transfixed on the guard. I saw the gold cross, dangling off to one side, and the trickle of blood leaking from the guard's ear. My mind was careening like a dark funnel cloud. Everything around me blurred.

"Let's go!" Harry yelled a second time.

Everyone in the cage who could still move came tumbling out. Those with gangrene from the long months of the chain cutting into their ankles looked on with disinterest. The rest began running down the dirt road, with me and Harry in the lead. When we heard the dogs coming after us, we ducked into the swamp. No one followed, believing the swamp, with its quicksand and adders, would be sure death. The other men preferred to take their chances on the chase. When we could no longer hear the dogs, me and Harry sunk down in the mud. The wet clay felt cool against the palms of my hands. I braced myself against sliding down the small embankment. The skunk cabbage smell was strong and, oddly, began to help clear my nausea. Harry, nearby, leaned against a stump, grabbed for me before I sank down too far into the muck.

The cloud cover made it so dark we couldn't see what was nearby.

"Shouldn't we keep moving?" I whispered.

"Maybe," Harry responded.

"Wouldn't we hear 'em with those dogs? I think they're gone."

"Let's wait an hour or so to be sure."

"Harry."

"Yeah?"

"I think I killed that guy back there."

"Well, it couldn't be helped."

I wanted to agree. The darkness had closed in on us. We shivered even though it was a warm, humid night. We heard a splash but couldn't see the water or what made the sound. I could only respond instinctively to Harry, to the dark, and to the animal sounds around us. The hair stood up on the back of my neck. Chills went down my spine.

For months we had all been chained together, the chains drawn tight between us so the closeness was mandatory and the stench of gangrene inescapable. When morning light came, the guard drug out the man on the end by his arms while the men directly behind screamed in pain from the festering sores where the chains had dug into their ankles. The rest of us rose from our knees and stood. We were caked from the dirt of road building. We would either die from gangrene or from a guard's head bashing. Then, a fresh supply of men would be brought in. Most of us were there for vagrancy.

The night before, I was chained next to Harry. We had spent the night whispering between the guard's rounds.

"The guard gets close enough for us to grab him," Harry whispered.

"Could you?" I said.

"Yeah, Harry answered.

"I reckon I could slide the bar loose and use it to knock him out."

"Make sure you really lay him out or we'll be dead." Harry's voice shook a little.

I didn't sleep after that. I thought of Mom and Pop, all the rest, and wondered whether they'd understand. I went over and over what I needed to do; I visualized the metal in my hand, the way to raise it overhead, the direction we needed to run. I remembered my rabbits being slaughtered, bits of bloody fur dropped into the dust. I shook my head to get rid of the image.

"Harry, do you think they'll ever catch up to us? What'll happen if they do?"

"I think you know what'll happen."

"I didn't mean to..."

"I know."

"They'd never believe that."

"They was killing us one by one." I tried to look over and see Harry but could barely see a shadow where he was.

"I can't be on the run all my life," I said.

"Then, what we gonna do?"

"Never tell anyone."

"I won't."

"Me neither."

"Are we criminals?"

"Maybe. I dunno."

We waited another hour in the swamp. I jolted, then edged over when I thought I felt a snake near my ankle. Harry had pulled his knees to his chest so his feet were out of the water.

"Harry, you still there?"

"Yeah."

"Are we gonna die?"

3 "A permanent solution to a temporary problem." — Anon

Suicide, self-destruction. "The severest form of self-criticism."
—Leonard Levinson
Roget's Super Thesaurus, Writer's Digest Books, 1995, p. 512.

2005, Katie, Seattle. Family secrets twist your insides. You try to tamp them down somewhere deep within. Buried memories cost something, though. They burn your energy keeping them down. There is some part of you that gets lost with the burying. You don't share that piece of yourself with anyone. Even Gerald doesn't know my father was a fugitive, though I've woken up beside him at least once a week for several years, now.

I look up at the high privacy window that stretches across one of the walls of Gerald's bedroom. The shades are always drawn. The drone of Seattle traffic disturbs me. Everything in the room is dark and masculine. The dresser is mahogany veneer. The headboard rises high up the wall and matches the dresser. The only decoration in the room is a large tray that holds change, tie clips, and wallet. At one time there was a photograph of a Northwest sunset that I had given him on the dresser, but it seems to have disappeared. I look at the plastic-covered white shirts, back from the cleaners and hung neatly on one side of the long closet. Below, three pairs of polished black shoes are lined up. Even though the walls are clinically white, they have turned gray in the dim light.

I've turned over towards Gerald, and he pulls me into his chest and kisses me hard and with lots of tongue. My neck clinches and spasms from the pressure. I have a headache and my back hurts. His hands find both my breasts and he moves the nipples with his thumbs and forefingers. I become moist. For a moment, my body doesn't seem to recall that my head aches and that my mind is in turmoil from the long sleepless night. I try to concentrate on sex.

All night I had mulled over Gerald's refusals. He had declined the invitation to attend my doctoral graduation ceremony. I had gone alone, all the way from Seattle to upstate New York, and was helped on with my robe by the secretary of my department. He always refuses to join me when I am meeting my friends. He never takes me along when he meets his friends. I feel the despair of being utterly alone, even though I feel Gerald's breath on my neck. It is the grip of loneliness I once had felt when I'd found myself a single parent, broke and in L.A.

His increasing movements, the tenseness in his back, jerk me into the present. He rolls off me and says, "Mmm...huh," a sound of pleasure as if he had just devoured a great meal.

"Do you want some coffee?" Gerald says.

I raise myself up and lean back on my elbows. "That would be great," I say with false enthusiasm.

"After I shower, I can drive you home."

Gerald drops me off at my house and we part with an awkward hug, leaning across the gear shift of his Volvo.

Once inside my house, I curl up on the chair at the vintage Formica table that sits under the casement windows in my tiny kitchen. I fiddle with my split ends. I look at the view of my neighbor's old-fashioned rose on a trellis. Gerald has only sat with me here twice, and both times he looked uncomfortable.

I tense my jaw, will myself to movement. I go down the back steps and out to the garage and grab the pickaxe. I will rip out the overgrown flower bed on the side of the house. I slam the metal into the dirt. Soil sprays onto my shoes and lodges in my pants cuffs. I bend down and rip at the trumpet vines. I soon have an armful of vines and weeds that I throw onto a pile on the lawn. I finish in a few hours, panting, and lean the pick axe against the fence. Then, I use the wheelbarrow to move everything onto the compost pile by the garage. Once I get all the tools put back into the garage, I take the back porch steps two at a time, grab my phone, sit down in the kitchen, and call my best friend, Audrey Blanchard.

"I have to go home this weekend and visit my parents' grave," I say. "It will be a break from Gerald, at least for a couple of days."

"What happened now?" Audrey asks.

"Gerald made plans with his friends, and as usual, he didn't include me. I don't understand...and he doesn't even take me to breakfast like he used to."

"Damn. Have you asked him why?"

"No. I can't bring myself to ask him. I'm sure he'd just give some lame excuse."

"I'm sorry. But do you think it will really help to go home?"

"I'm not sure. I've just got to get away. Escape."

"Well, it's not a bad idea to get out of town. But, man, I'd never let a guy sink his claws into me like you have Gerald. Are you sure that's what you want?"

I don't know how to respond. I want to defend Gerald but I can't. After a pause, I say, "Well, enough about me. What's going on for you?"

"Not much. No one's likely to rile me, the way Gerald does you. I just call my man when I'm in the mood, and, they'd better hurry because some-times the mood doesn't last long." Audrey laughs, a melodic sound that fits with her elegant style. "Just call me when you get back." Even though Audrey always says she doesn't need a regular romantic interest in her life, prefers to have a fling now and then, I always wonder if that's true. And she certainly could have anyone she wants. A former model, she is beautiful in that classic French way, like the actress Audrey Tautou. To add to her exotic good looks, she even speaks and teaches French!

"Oh, someone will get to you someday," and I laugh, too. Audrey always helps me lighten up. But this time that isn't enough. I've got to go home. There's a rush of adrenaline when I hang up. I dash through the house, throwing pajamas, extra jeans, and T-shirts out on a chair. I jerk my suitcase from underneath the bed, where it's hidden behind an eyelet ruffle. I slam everything, partially folded, and some rolled, into the case.

I toss a large grocery bag filled with sunflowers and dahlias from my yard into the back seat. I steel myself against the blast of heat as I open the front door and slide in under the steering wheel.

Once on I-5, I feel about the debris on the passenger seat until I locate my crumpled baseball cap, stuff my hair under it to keep it from whipping into my face, and run both windows down. The air feels cool on my damp T-shirt and drifts across my bare feet in flip flops. Wind scatters through the car, fluttering the assorted student papers on the seat beside me onto the floor, reminding me I should have returned them before this weekend.

Especially Carrie Anderson's personal essay on top. I make a vow to edit it and get it back to her on Monday. Students like Carrie often touch me. They come from a gritty background, in Carrie's case, the Oakland projects, and they have seen too much too soon. I see that flicker of pain in their eyes. Sometimes they talk about what that pain is about and sometimes they don't. I'm told I'm a good listener, that I have empathy. That pleases me. My background is different but there is something there in Carrie's eyes that I relate to.

Carefully keeping my eyes on the road, I lean over and slide my backpack down onto the papers to anchor them. I am relieved when I get past Olympia, and the traffic, along with the exhaust fumes, begins to thin.

I turn left at the White Pass exit. I am now heading east, calmed by the pungency of silage and freshly mowed hay. Familiar smells.

Recollections creep up on me, hard on the heels of a gentle summer shower from a single cloud overhead. Large rain drops splat on my windshield and trickle down through the dust as I get closer to home.

Katie Nolan

It was 1955. I sat in the car with my father, for more than an hour, while he babysat and amused me by having me watch the rain drops on the windows of the car. We set them against one another in a race. Sometimes one drop would merge with the other, so there wasn't any way to call the winner. The windows steamed up and reduced the world to our interior space. Before I knew it, my mother's grocery shopping was done, and we were on our way back home, across the Cowlitz River bridge, back to Green Mountain.

These memories of my father remind me of how bereft I felt when I lost him. I often visualize how I will stand by my parents' shared gravestone and finally double over in grief, weeping beautifully like Vivien Leigh in "Gone With the Wind."

Once at the cemetery, I crouch down by my parents' shared stone. Clarence R. Nolan, born, 1914. Natalie E. Nolan, born, 1920. The stone is slate-colored with flecks of pink and tiny sparkles that mimic fool's gold. A heart between their names graces the center of the stone, and carved on it is "Married, November 2, 1941." Giant northwest firs circle the periphery of the cemetery. Stone markers in the firs' shadows form a cluster of graves of infants and children. Some have tiny angel wings above the name. Baby Spencer, 1920-1920, Remus Spencer, 1914-1915, George Sheridan Belcher, 1908-1911. Family names that have been in the area for generations. Many of them are distant relatives to my cousins. I breathe slowly as I wander about and look at them, feeling sad that they never got to live their lives.

The caretaker has mowed the rough meadow of scruffy grass and dandelions. I slow my walk to keep my balance on the dips and rolls.

This time, like many others, I do not weep like Vivien Leigh in "Gone with the Wind." I do not weep like anyone. I only go numb looking at my parents' carved and polished stone.

I stumble back to my car. I sit for a moment, mesmerized by the sun's glare on the lake below. The lake is framed by ragged pasture in front and a high ridge of firs and alders behind. An alder closer by has been attacked by caterpillars so its browned leaves are full of holes and dropping to the ground. I start the engine. I notice the mingled smell of gasoline and sun-heated pine needles.

14

I glance back in my rear-view mirror at the dirt and gravel road that leads to the cemetery. The flowers I'd brought are wilting, forgotten, in the back seat.

I once had faith that someone besides my father would love me unconditionally. It would be signified by romantic passion and ignorance of my flaws. I believed that I would leave home as soon as I graduated from high school. I felt no shame for our tar paper shack that had neither phone nor T.V. nor indoor plumbing. Most of these amenities wouldn't come along until I was fourteen. But I still wanted to leave as soon as possible.

I had a whole childhood set up on dreams. I wanted to replace the shack with a simple farmhouse of my own, one with all the modern conveniences, preferably with a large yard with a picket fence. Several children would be playing in front of the house. There would be a barnyard dotted with Holstein cows and a shepherd curled up on the front porch. A sensitive and powerful man completed the picture. Someone who picked me up, laughing, and carried me in his arms through the house, the way my father had my mother.

The dream all went down like a rickety barn in a hurricane force gale when I got married at eighteen and discovered that Wayne Woodson had no intention of carrying out his promise that we would build such a life together. Trust in the future eroded further when Wayne began to make fun of how I dressed (which admittedly was a bit too casual with my baggy jeans and his old T-shirts), and when he assured me that I didn't have the sense that God gave a goose. Something inside of me clicked off when he laughed at how I looked naked. I had shaved my pubic hair in hopes that he would be as en-amored of me as he seemed to be of the Playboy centerfold. When he didn't stop laughing, I fled from the room and choked down silent sobs in the closet down the hall.

I haven't come far, even though I divorced Wayne decades ago. I've studied feminism so that I no longer shave anything. Nor do I compare my-self to Bunnies. Yet, I still want to escape. Gerald. My job. Everything.

* * *

It is only a short distance between the cemetery and the Cowlitz River bridge. I drive across the bridge feeling a bit nauseous, the way I often do after I drink too much coffee. I feel the cool wind coming up off the water. I imagine myself descending, into that coolness, car smashing through the railing. Me and the crate of metal falling into the watery abyss. My heart thudding, I jerk my head away from the edge, and veer the car from the walkway back into my lane. I hold tight to the steering wheel with both hands and concentrate on the white lines on the road.

Oh my god! Would I really do this? Did I just think this? I cannot entertain such thoughts. I'm trained to be a survivor. My hands shake as they grip the wheel.

I wonder whether this is how it happens. The people who jump off bridges. They find themselves teetering on the edge, a dull ache throughout their bodies. No adrenaline. No clear thoughts. Then, they either fall, or with their mental reign of terror, actually jump. Are they borne on the wind or would they drop straight down? I've heard that suicides suddenly realize their mistake in the midst of falling, and that terrifies me.

I've always thought that it would be best to do something dramatic, anything, rather than to carry out the suicidal thoughts. Go to a remote part of the globe. Camp on a tropical beach. Do anything! What if I simply turned left on I-5? Went south, on and on, through southern California, across the border into Mexico, all the way down into Central America, then into South America, to disappear into an unknown world. I'd change my name, create an identity, and begin anew.

4 Bird of Passage

Phrase meaning traveller: 268,
Roget's Thesaurus, 1947.

The third Nolan commandment, Thou shalt never grieve.

August, 2009, Katie, Seattle to Portland. I sit in my assigned seat, gray-green to match the carpet. I stare at the station's backside as the train lumbers forward. I try on my new name, Katie Nolan.

I form my name, silently moving my lips. I like it. Distractedly, I stare downward, lips parted to form a k, avoiding the eyes of those seeing off loved ones. There is gritty cracked asphalt sloping down to the tracks, both damp from the light drizzle. Next to the asphalt, cobblestone walkway gives way to poured cement then cement gives up to cobblestone again. The cobblestone was likely there when my father came through this station in the 1930s.

I'd prefer to think about my father's life during this period of time, the Great Depression. But for the moment, all I can think about is his death. I thought when he died, it would be an exception to the Nolan commandment, that there is no time to grieve. I thought I might crumple to the ground and wail. Sit on thorns. Call out, Woe is me! Be like the biblical Job in sackcloth and ashes. I didn't call out and I wasn't like Job. All I felt was a sense of disinterest. Disinterest in those around me, disinterest in activities, sometimes disinterest in myself.

Even Gerald notices that there is something unsaid about my father. "You talk about him as if he is still alive," he says to me one day, after I've told him about my Dad being attacked by railroad bulls. Gerald's voice is accusing and puzzled, but he isn't the kind of person to ask questions.

A few weeks ago, I told Audrey that I wanted to find my father somehow, on this rail pass. See what he saw, travel where he travelled, try to understand what happened. When Audrey asked me what I meant by "finding my father" and "try to be interested again," I was not able to give her an explanation. How can I explain something I don't understand?

Nor have I expressed to Audrey just how desperate I felt as I planned my journey. When I tried to explain my problem to her, I completely blanked out and was overcome with a sense of sadness. I couldn't tell her of my suicidal thoughts. Nor could I tell her I might not return. I've read that if you do not have a carefully planned out method for suicide, then it is not the big worry. I don't. Although, occasionally, more often than I care to admit, I wonder how it would be to veer off the road over a cliff. But doesn't everyone wonder?

* * *

Gerald says he is too busy to take me to the train station. Saturday, he says, and didn't I remember, is his day to run errands, get to the cleaners, pay bills, go to the bank.

Years ago he had patiently explained to me the reason he had to pay his bills in person. It was because as a black man he was treated badly at the bank, not allowed to withdraw his money unless he not only gave all his proper identification but also subjected himself to fingerprinting! Then, he had to see the manager and felt the indignity of being treated like a common criminal when he protested that he had been with the bank for two years. After that, he vowed to never use a checking account again, keeping only a savings account at the teachers' credit union.

So I am making my way downtown on the Seattle Metro, feeling abandoned. Why does Gerald do things for me I don't need done and never show up when I need him? I sigh.

Gerald's image looms large. I try to be understanding. At the same time I feel frustrated at his seeming oblivion to my needs, I am drawn to his six foot frame, and his wit and laughter, that sometimes pulls us both in until we are laughing our heads off. When I observe him around other people, he is usually aloof and regal, so, when he pays attention to them, it makes them feel special. It seems he never lets down and just unwinds with others. He is not the type of person who could relax enough with his students, for example, to accept a nickname like Ger. He remains Mr. Gerald Hardwick, or just Mr. Hardwick, to his students. No exceptions.

I sigh again. Today, he is not going to pay any attention to me at all. I wait for Metro, glancing at my watch. In spite of the late bus, and with some relief, I notice I have thirty minutes to spare in catching the train to Portland, then, Los Angeles. Breathless, I take my place at the end of a long line that snakes out the entry door of the train station, leaving the last stragglers standing in the Seattle drizzle.

I inch forward in line for twenty minutes, awkwardly pushing my luggage with my foot. Once inside, I notice the architect's images of the tin ceiling and the ancient chandeliers. It pleases me that they are renovating this old station. That soon the lowered ceiling will be removed and will reveal these architectural treasures.

I shiver because the back of my jeans jacket is damp. The fronts of my jeans are damp, too, and feel like they are sticking to my thighs. My feet are freezing. Even though it is summer, I should have worn my winter boots and wool socks, instead of these tennis shoes.

Finally, I file out Door 3, and glance at the people around me. If they are going the distance, they carry a blanket and pillow. My bedding is attached with Bungee cords on the outside of my battered suitcase, the same one I have used for years to roll books and students' papers between philosophy classes. The bedding slips down precariously as I struggle up the steps to Car 14, carrying my laptop in a canvas bag with a wide strap pressing against my shoulder. I now pull the medium-sized wheeled suitcase with one hand, and grapple with the overnight bag with my other hand, while trying to push the slipping strap of my laptop case back up my shoulder. The overnight bag is heavy with journals. I have lugged all these notebooks along on this trip, many of which I have not looked at for decades.

19

My writing teacher at Hugo House in Seattle, Mickey Dillinger, has encouraged me to take the time to look back. Gather these vignettes in the notebooks about my father and write them down in a coherent story. Of course Mickey doesn't know the specific details. I'm just not ready to share them, perhaps out of habit, but also out of fear of judgement.

I'm on the train! Escape at last! I am going south and I do not know where I'm going to end up. I write in my journal, pushing hard on its binding to flatten it onto the seat back tray.

I am excited, I continue writing, *and I imagine myself embarking on a Kerouac-type adventure. But if truth be told, I am not really the exotic or romantic type. I have a tendency to be stuck in a practical survival mode. Yet, I want to hear a conductor shout "All aboard!" I loved those pictures in my fifth grade social studies book of train conductors in uniform and cap, smiling, hanging on to the curved metal bar, and leaning out of the door of a train car. "All aboard!" Not a sound. Just the gentle hum of the air conditioner inside the car and the quiet voices of other passengers getting settled into the upholstered seats.*

I stand up to shove my suitcase overhead to make room for my seat mate, a young woman wearing stylishly torn jeans and ear buds, then collapse back onto the seat and rest my feet on the little square bag full of memories, a 1950s blue overnight case that was my mother's. There is a mirror just inside the lid with a blue ruffled cord holding it in place.

The inside of the case is covered with sky-blue rayon, silky and soothing to my hands, where last night I had placed and stacked the journals done up in composition notebooks. I have always used these little composition notebooks for my journal, after carefully thinking through what would work the best. They are perfect in their smaller size, available everywhere, and lack a metal spiral which tends to get wound into either another notebook in my backpack or into some clothing or other, snagging it.

These are the notebooks that carry my, and my family's past. I need them for my memory. Because events that occur, especially if they are traumatic in any way, are tamped down, perhaps in some sort of memory vault buried thrice. Once, when you realize that you cannot share them with any-one. Again, when you don't want them to remove all chance for tranquility. And, finally, when you manage a way to almost remove them from memory such that *it is as if the event never happened.*

As I stare out the window at the cold metal of the tracks below, their silver tones matching the smooth, sullen gray of low clouds, I think about my father being abandoned to the rails by Grandma and Grandpa Nolan. Well, not really abandoned. Many young men, boys really, rode the rails in the 1930s. It was the only way they could find work after the Stock Market Crash.

Of course my father was no longer riding the rails when I was born in 1947. But in the years 1928 to 1941, he was a working hobo, jumping the "side-car coaches," interacting with the communists and the Wobblies, who were organizing along the lines. With the exception of a short stint as a soldier in the Philippines, he was on the road the entire time. Finally, he left his fourteen years of hobo life behind when he was twenty-seven and met my mother.

So, is this search for my father going to help me find the origin of my troubles with relationships? I jot this question down in my journal and underline it several times.

I know when we start tracing the origin of something it can go back further than we can imagine—to the first evolutionary humans, for instance, or even to an infinite regress. Some say that we are genetically hardwired to be caught up in the snares of love gone awry. But if that is the case, why do others seemingly have a love relationship that lasts more than half a century, as evidenced by those fiftieth anniversary plates edged with gold? And why can't I point, with great assurance, to a moment when I fell in love with someone, so that I, too, being human, would have a chance for love to go awry?

When I've asked my friends how one knows when they fall in love, they always say, "Oh, you'll know." And Audrey usually adds, "I'm not so sure I really want to fall in love again." But I don't know. I have no clue how Gerald feels about me and I am confused about how I feel about him.

21

Well, I suppose Gerald did try to express his feelings. Early on he asked me to marry him and said he loved me. I don't know why, but I just couldn't use the *love* word. And I always put him off about marriage, joking that "I'm not the marryin' kind."

These seemingly unanswerable questions about love, naked and naive, and as if sprung from deep in the earth below the rails, or from nowhere, leap up from the tracks and assail me. Like life itself, which, I've often felt as hollow. Never enjoying dinners and parties. Waiting for them to end. Feeling nothing while I try to look after the feelings of others. Waiting until I can be alone again to replenish my energy. Lately, I've neither looked forward to lovemaking nor to parties, yet I've participated in both.

Delicious not to be bound to stifling routines. Time to write, of which I'd had precious little. This was not only due to my friends, family and full-time job teaching philosophy, but also to my commitments to various groups, such as Fellowship of Reconciliation, and Malik Rahim's, Common Ground of New Orleans, a grassroots effort to rebuild New Orleans after Hurricane Katrina. The train is a haven, away from the reality of war, poverty and injustice, a perfect place to write, with few available distractions.

I am on the Coast Starlight, which leaves from Seattle going south, mornings and afternoons. I love everything about this train. It has a large lounge car that is light and bright, scenery that surrounds you due to the wrap-a-round windows that begin at your feet and curve cathedral-like over-head, allowing you to look up and see sky and treetops. With the tracks at my feet and the trees so close, I feel slightly dizzy as the trees whizz by. The train rolls through a tunnel near Tacoma, the tunnel's curved entry framed at the bottom by stacked rocks. The late afternoon rays peek through billowing clouds and blind the passengers sitting on the right side of the train as we exit the other end. Wet leaves glisten and the sun flashes past the leaves creating little patches of light and shadow on the ground. We roll along the water of Puget Sound, where I observe two great blue herons, their long patient legs holding them as still as a zen master. Motionless, they watch for fish.

Travel can be a form of amnesia, suspending one in stillness, obliterating the past. My mind tends to float away when I travel.

It would be so easy for me to get caught up in the details of my trip and lose my focus. Restless, I push at the blue case with my feet and vow: I *will* fight against this. I *will* remember everything about my family's past, no matter how painful. I will write it all down.

I am giving my father a new name because it is just too disturbing to face the trauma of his struggle without making it less real by pretending he is someone else. I've tried to avoid feeling this pain by speaking of it from afar. Perhaps I'll try the distance of the omniscient voice I've learned about in writing class. No. There is too much I don't know. Perhaps first person will be easier.

I can make some effort to get inside his consciousness. So, maybe I'm writing, not actually about Bud Nolan, but my memory of him.

My father once told me he had always avoided this Seattle-Portland route after the first time, having come close to getting wiped off the top of the train in the tunnel. It is difficult to conjure up an image of riding fearfully on the top, while I sit in the lounge car sipping my wine, my feet propped on a little shelf. I wish to consider how it felt to deck a train, whether riding on top or inside. No. My thoughts betray me, jump to Gerald. Can't I just focus on the hobos?

Alas. I find myself holding my head in my hands, as if pressing on it will cause some idea to gel, or push it away from this distraction. It doesn't work. Then, I want an epiphany so that I can make a decision about Gerald once and for all. Because there is no worse place to be than when one is indecisive about a relationship. I need the relief of a decision. Should I try again with Gerald? Should I go back to Seattle? Should I return to my old life at all?

I had similar questions when my first husband, Wayne, called after me, "What's wrong with you, anyway?" There's always Gerald, or some other guy, yelling after me. With Gerald, in particular, because we break up often. We went on a trip to Canada a few weeks ago, which led to our most recent split.

* * *

"Let's stop here," Gerald had said.

We are at the Canadian border just north of Bellingham. I wait in the car, his white Volvo with taupe leather seats. My baggy white shorts would be comfortable except that the backs of my legs are sticking to the leather.

23

The interior smells faintly of his musky cologne. He always has his car detail-cleaned when he takes it in for regular maintenance. Oddly, I both appreciate and am disturbed by its immaculate perfection. I enjoy the pristine environment but it also causes me to feel inexplicably anxious. Perhaps, because it makes me think he wants a model of a woman and not this occasionally dirty and smelly, real woman in the flesh? I sometimes feel like flaunting my sweaty and dirt-streaked skin, right after I have pursued my passion of backyard organic gardening, just to see him turn away.

In a few moments he comes back with a bottle of duty-free Chivas Regal. Okay, I'm thinking. He is not my first husband. Men always accuse me of assigning them traits they don't have. "Must have been that other guy you were with because that's not me," they say.

That other guy, my first husband, who became an alcoholic. When we were first married, we played pool and darts in the neighborhood bar. Then our first child arrived, and he stopped coming home from work.

Is Gerald the same? I really know how to pick 'em. Another alcoholic! No! He has only bought a bottle of whiskey. That does not make him an alcoholic. I will just wait and see.

Later that night, glass after glass on the rocks, the entire bottle is upended beside the bed in our Vancouver B.C. hotel room. I sit stiffly beside him, pillow propped sideways against the headboard. My back aches from my awkward position.

It is a charming hotel, really, where they have maximized the 1960s architecture, played it out to the full by putting bedspreads on the beds with wild orange and brown geometric patterns, with dashes of black. An orange plastic stool cozies up to a well-polished 1950s waterfall dresser. There is interesting art on the wall that reminds me of Escher prints. But I feel ill, unable to truly appreciate the kitschy charm, even though I haven't had anything to drink.

It is pure torture as I watch him get drunk, holed up against the bed cushions in his boxer shorts and gray T-shirt. The T.V. screen flashes pictures that I do not see, and I only absorb the drone of voices and the shifts from commercials to program. I flee. I decide to drag my suitcase to the second bedroom of the suite, lift it against my thigh so the wheels won't squeak and give me away. Then, after a restless few hours, knowing he is in the other room passed out, I flee again.

I've shed my pajamas for jeans and a T-shirt and I slink quietly out the door of the hotel room, inch the suitcase along so as not to wake him, relieved when I make it to the lobby. Will he wake up and try to find me? I both hope he will and hope he won't. I sit in the lobby and try to decide what to do.

After a distressing few hours sunk into the lobby's overstuffed couch and leaning against one of its huge rolled arms, I take the Trailways bus back to Seattle. The tour director is explaining to the busload of retired couples that they would be in Seattle in three hours and would have a two hour lay-over before their cruise. Am I the only one not going?

"Why did you leave?" Gerald says plaintively, when he calls.

"It upset me when you drank all that whiskey. I've told you before that's what my first husband did. It still upsets me when someone drinks a lot." I try to explain myself, make sure I sound even-handed and rational. I can imagine him sitting, smug and comfortable in his favorite leather chair, in the living room of his split level back in Seattle, or if he's still in Canada, sitting in the rolled arm chair in the room. I don't ask him where he is. I speak quietly on my cell phone to avoid disturbing the people around me on the bus.

"Well, you could have handled it differently." The tone in his voice seems to end the conversation, and I accept fault for ruining what was supposed to be a pleasure trip.

* * *

Wait! I am going south to L.A. not north to Canada! I am going in the opposite direction. That has to mean something. At least, I am relieved to be on the train.

I will focus on *this* journey—I shake my head vigorously and shrug my shoulders to help rearrange my thoughts. I place my pen on the seat back tray and retrieve my journal from the floor, where it slipped when the train lurched forward. It frightens me to even think about what I am proposing to do.

25

5 Pleased with a Feather, Tickled with a Straw

Phrase meaning amusement, also on the light fantastic toe,
rompish, playful as a kitten: 840,
Roget's Thesaurus, 1947.

The fourth Nolan commandment, Thou shalt always appear calm.

2009, Katie, Portland to Los Angeles. I am heading to Los Angeles where
it rarely snows. The lack of seasons in southern California changes time and
makes it drift. The nine years I spent there, married to my first husband,
Wayne, and in my twenties, I lived within a psychological haze that matched
the smog. I flew home that first Christmas after we separated.

* * *

On Green Mountain, the air was sharp and clear, and the snow fell
as if time had no essence. Big flakes that made children happy. That made
me happy. Dry, too, so your feet slipped through it like air. It was the kind of
snow that required children to pack it down with rubber barn boots, walking
side by side up the hill, stomping it down lightly. Once packed it allowed the
Radio Flyer to glide, at first a slow crunch through the snow, then faster and
faster as it gained momentum.

The entire family had returned for Christmas. It was 1975, so we
arrived wearing an abundance of polyester. Nattie, my mother, fully expected
all of us to be there every year, and we usually were, even though we had

to travel from as far away as California to get to the old farm nestled in the foothills of the Cascades on the western side of the mountains.

I arrived last from Los Angeles. I loved going home, visiting the barn where I'd played, seeing Mount Rainier peeking above the clouds, the clue that I was almost within spitting distance from home. Yet, visits home also brought on this discomfort I felt with my mother. I'd always had to keep things from her because she could be so judgemental. That had worn on me.

For one thing, there was this secret between myself and my father. Dad was a fugitive, although I seldom thought of him that way. And of course, no one else in the family thought about it either, because no one else knew.

An easy warmth existed between my father and me. Did my mother notice this? Feel left out somehow? I never knew and never had the courage to ask. Well, it isn't really something you can ask someone. I wondered if a couple that loves each other can be close in spite of a secret or two? And my parents did love each other, of that I was certain.

"Will you build us a big bonfire?" I asked Dad.

"You mean at the top of the hill?" Dad nodded towards the knoll at the top of the forty acre pasture, the same field where he'd spread grass seed with me years ago.

"I'll help carry up some wood. We can get a good one going."

"Okay," he answered, and grinned, likely remembering the bonfires, the hot chili afterwards, the shouts of excited children. I too, recalled my mother's homemade cinnamon rolls, the hot cocoa, along with the chili, all crowded on the back of the wood stove.

The wood cooking stove no longer there, it had been long since replaced by an electric one. The wood heater sat next to the electric stove, though, as if the kitchen had been required to retain its nod to the past.

My father sat next to the wood stove, on a chrome-legged chair backwards, with his feet wrapped around the chair's legs and his chest pressing against the back of the chair, so he was facing the stove. This was his usual position in the morning. The grandkids began trooping into the kitchen, excited by the sight of snow outside.

"Let's try out the skis I got at the Goodwill," Dad said. So we all did. It was pleasant for us, the three siblings, to share with our own kids what we had known growing up. Now, Bud and Nattie had five grandchildren in all. Two each from my brother and sister, and, the one from me.

We managed to get the skis to stay attached to our feet, even though we had no ski boots and strapped on the skis using some baling twine to get them to hold tight to our rubber barn boots. I started down the hill first. I relished the feeling of speeding down the slope, sliding my makeshift skis around mounds in the pasture. My brother, David, followed, not wanting to be outdone in front of his daughters, Melanie and Samantha. He beat me to the bottom and chuckled when my ski caught on an icy ridge and I went down, laughing, having made it only halfway to the flat part of the pasture below.

Dad stayed behind to show the grandkids how to maneuver their special skis. He grinned at his granddaughters, Melanie, Samantha, and Sarah, as they giggled at his teasing. He would tug on whatever ponytail was within reach, at the moment the dog barked, then ask them why their tail was barking. "Oh, Grandpa," they would say. Then, off they went, headed down the hill, grandfather and five grandchildren following. They all whooped and laughed as they fell in the soft snow, not quite getting the hang of it their first try.

Bud trudged slowly back up the hill, awkward in the skis and rubber boots. He lifted up the granddaughters one by one and set them on their feet. Then, the two grandsons, Jonathan (my son) and Robert (my sister's son). "Grandpa, Grandpa, show us again how to do it!" They all clamored for another lesson in "rubber boot" skiing.

"Well, ya gotta concentrate. Don't think about nothin' else. Don't look down at your feet. Keep your eyes a couple of feet in front of you, scanning further down now and then. Don't think too much about it or you'll get all tangled up. You have to trust the snow. It'll let you glide along." He had applied his knowledge of how to do the impossible and deck a moving freight to this odd skiing. "Okay. Let's try 'er again!"

One of the granddaughters, Melanie, got it first. She flew down the hill, making it all the way to the level bottom, and needing to sit down hard, lest she go over a little ledge that dropped to the creek. Bud smiled with pride at giving a successful lesson.

Back at the top, exhilarated, the grandchildren all stripped off their gloves and began to warm their hands on the big bonfire. Sarah and Samantha rushed up the hill, away from the fire, to make snow angels. Dad looked up at them with a grandfather's pride. Past them, he could see the spring that he had tapped almost thirty years earlier, so an abundant flow of water had supplied the farmhouse in the little hollow below.

The water had been as prolific as our father's gentle teasing. He never failed to think of something. One time he would make a strange sound, like a frog, then he'd blame us for croaking. "Who's that croaking?" he'd ask, and look from one of us to the other. Or he would do the classic sleight of hand and find a nickel behind our ear.

"Oh, Grandpa. Tell us again about riding the rails." All of the grandkids loved his stories. No grandfather could measure up to his heroic charm and indulgent humor. At least, that is the way his children and grandchildren saw it.

"Oh, ya really wanna know?" He always enjoyed telling his grandkids about his life on the rails. "I rode the rattlers," he'd say and chuckle. He may have even told them about getting vagged but Grandma Nattie made sure he stopped short of jail stories. "That'd be a bad influence! Don't you tell them that!" she'd call out, whenever it seemed he might have forgotten.

"Well, it wasn't legal, ya know, but lots of people did it those days," was Grandpa's defense. As his stories were told and retold, the heaviness of his distant past seemed to be lost in time.

I heard it first. "Hey, someone is at the door!" I called out. I was further back in the house, but my parents didn't hear that well, so I was the first to notice the insistent knocking. Dad got up to answer, after both Mom and Dad had shouted out their usual "Halloo! Come on in!"

Strangers seldom knocked in this remote place, so they assumed it was one of the neighbors or more family. When they didn't come in, Dad shrugged and ambled off to answer the door. He opened it, mumbling, "Why don't they just come on in?"

29

Dad glanced back at me. I took in a sharp, deep breath because the men had on uniforms. Dad turned toward me again and gave me a hard look. It meant calm down. I looked down at my feet.

It was the FBI. My stomach sank. They've caught up with him. Seeing him taken off to prison, a vise grip surrounded my chest, followed by a thud in my temple. I became nauseous. I tried to keep my gaze steady on my feet.

"Can we talk with you a minute?" There were two of them. The one who spoke did not smile. His partner glanced around the room as if looking for evidence. Their black uniforms were mussed; they likely had travelled a long distance.

"Sure," Dad said.

There was nowhere to go. My heart raced. I took in a shallow breath, held it.

"Someone's been shooting at planes flying overhead. Through this valley. Do you have any idea who that is?" The FBI agent was asking my father this question, but he peered around my father and noticed me fidgeting by the stove. Then, both trained their attention on my father.

"Well, I dunno. But I've heard people talking 'bout a crazy guy over yonder. Maybe has some problems from Vietnam." Dad gestured to the left, indicating where the neighbor lived.

The few scattered people around the foothills often wondered who was shooting into the air. Shots were heard whenever the pilots from McChord Air Force base did maneuvers up our valley, a valley that meandered high into the Cascades, stopping abruptly at the source for Sulphur Creek.

"Thanks. If you hear any more let us know." And they each handed him a card. Then, they turned and walked back across the yard. They were chatting quietly. Each nodded occasionally.

Maybe they weren't after my father. Or was it just an investigative trick? A fishing expedition. That meant they would be back. How can my father appear so calm?

My mind jumped between my father's words. *"Don't tell no one 'til I'm dead."* The words he'd used when he'd told me his secret. *"Can't trust no one."* Words that crept up on me. *"Even Nat don't know."*

Thoughts continued to race. Chaotic like whitecaps on Riffe Lake at the foot of Green Mountain. Blowing this way and that. I anguished over the idea that they would come back. Would they put him in prison? Losing him that way was unimaginable.

Please, I whispered to myself. Then bit my lower lip and let out my breath. Please. No.

6 On the Wing

Locomotion by water or air: 267,
Roget's Thesaurus, 1947.

2009, Katie, Portland to Los Angeles. In my journal it says "bicycle sail-ing." I glance down at the great Columbia River. We are on the bridge that separates Washington and Oregon, and I marvel at the expanse below, the ocean-going freighters, the occasional coal barge. Seagulls have made their multiple gray-white marks along the metal arches.

Filmy patches of blue swim in the gray sky above. It would be difficult to sail this river, I muse. The faint rumble of wheels on track are soothing.

* * *

I was in my thirties, visiting home, waiting to hear another of my father's stories, when his mood changed. He looked rather serious then cleared his throat.

He put his hand on one knee of his navy-blue polyester slacks, hemmed by my mother's hand and slightly too short. His sparkling hazel eyes changed shade depending on the color of his shirt. On this day, his eyes were quite green. He was wearing a green and blue plaid flannel with an extra button-down pocket my mother had sewn on the front for his wallet because, since his hobo days, he had always avoided keeping cash in his back pants pocket.

He looked up at the ceiling as if searching for the event in his memory. It was morning and the kitchen had east-facing windows. The flood of light from the sun peering over the Cascade mountains seemed to cause him to become his usual cheerful self again.

Leisurely, my father began in his Irish story-telling fashion. He sometimes regaled me with the poetic language of his Irish ancestors, immigrants who settled in the South in the 1800s. They had created a mixture of Irish brogue and southern slang, a dialect they carried with them when they fled north during the Civil War, the boys (including my Great Grandpa Nolan) running alongside the wagon in the trees so as not to be conscripted into the Confederate army.

1928, Bud, near Arapahoe, Nebraska. Chores done, school out, I felt a wee bit antsy. I was looking at pictures of sailing vessels in an old stereoscope and imagined sailing on one of them. The varnished oak of the sides of the stereoscope felt smooth on m' hands, as I slid them along the scope to adjust it so that it flooded each picture with light. Mr. Northby at the ranch nearby had given me some pictures of tropical islands, including ones of the Philippines, a place that Mr. Northby had gone when he was in the army. I dreamt of sailing there, imagined swaying palms, women in hula hula skirts, and sandy ocean beaches. That's how I got the idea that a sail could be rigged up on m'bicycle. That's the day I went sailing.

Dad paused at this point in his story and grinned widely. He got up and stretched, then sat back down on the chrome-legged chair, facing it toward the table this time.

"A sail on a bicycle? That really works?" I asked.

"Yep," he answered, and grinned some more.

The wind pushed me along, through cover crops of rye, past the mill pond, past the crossroads. I must've been doing thirty, forty! The road was a hard-packed two-lane with a mound in the middle where dust blew around the dandelions and chickweed. I breathed in deeply, barely missing the garden snake that slid into the ditch. I felt almost free. Free from shucking the corn. Free from tension at home, related to the threat that the bank was a'goin' to take the place. Free from the low voices at night that turned into shouting and blame: "If you'd stop drinking some of that rum, you'd be paying more attention. What are we going to do? We should have sold when we had a chance…" And Mom went on this way for god knows how long. Then Pop said something, quietly, so's it don't come through the walls. Then, Mom starts in again. I was free from all that and felt happy. But my little bit of joy didn't last long.

With a start I read the peeling sign, "Arapahoe, 5 miles." I'd sailed eighty-five miles and now I was a'goin to catch hell if found out. But when I turned the bike for home, the wind had died down. Even the crickets got quiet in the wind's being gone. The bicycle sail was dead weight now but I kept it, hoping the wind would return. Nothing left to do but pedal home. The clouds became pink, then stars, but I still pedalled and pedalled.

I pedalled for what seemed like God's own eternity, thistle-down floating into my face, brushing across my forehead, barely noticed, because all I could think about was the beating I was gonna get when I got home. The moon was bright, almost full, as I kept on pedalling. I met no one, was only viewed by cows, curious, ambling toward the fence, stopping to look on. I pedalled for one hour, then two, then slowed as one leg seized up. That pain made me brake hard, dismount, and tumble into the ditch, shallow and dry, next to the pasture.

The smell of ragweed and dry dust caused my eyes to water as I lay there, waiting for the cramp to go away. The ragweed set me to sneezing. As the cramp went away, I was kinda teched by the three-quarters moon. It didn't usually affect me that way. I felt a little lonely. Maybe 'cause of the cradling moonlight.

It'd be good to be happy and free but I hadn't seen anyone like that. Sure not in my family. Maybe down the road apiece, I had seen a family that bantered happily over supper. It was Mr. Northby's just a mile down from us. That's what I'd like. Just the daily, happy banter. And that's when I vowed that I was gonna get my own ranch and start my own family, see to it that nobody was yelling.

I fell asleep, damp from sweat, and woke up chilled to the bone in spite of the warm evening, the cows still looking in on me by the side of the road. Lying on my back in the ditch, I looked up and saw a hawk soaring overhead, the jagged tips of its wings spraying the first rays of morning sunlight. I was wishing I could be free like the hawk, not bound to earth, where it feels heavy, at times, as if a man is crushed under a mound of soil. Imagining just how it feels 'cause I'd had to bury my dog just a week before, mounding the soil over the stiff body, one shovelful at a time. So I dreamt I was up there, close to the sun, looking things over down below, buildings like small dots, and fields in their checker-board patterns.

I woke up hungry and thirsty, but been taught to pay no attention to either and just keep goin'. Any complaints regarding hunger or thirst had always been met with: "Well, that's just too bad. What a pity! Hang it! So are the rest of us, but you don't see us a bitchin' and a moanin'."

So I got up and pedalled hard.

Dad stopped for a minute and looked at me. I was nodding, alert, encouraging. I noticed the multi-paned kitchen windows that had not been changed since I was a toddler. Only the curtains had shifted from red-checked ones to cafe' curtains, bordered with picket fences with sunflowers mingled with blue johnny-jump-ups, poking through the fence slats. A blue wall clock shaped like a frying pan, complete with handle, matched the blue plastic upholstery on the chairs. The clock registered six in the morning. The blue and white wallpaper I'd pasted on with my mother was dotted with tiny colonial-style houses. There was the faint smell of wood smoke blended with the aroma of Folger's coffee.

Dad continued telling his story.

When I finally arrived I tried to inch past the porch and out to the barn without being caught. If'n I just slipped into morning chores, and if my brothers kept quiet, I maybe can avoid the wrath of my mother and the beating by Pop.

I saw Pop out of the corner of m'eye, stomping down the porch steps, one foot hitting harder than the other because he had sprained an ankle that had never healed right. One of Pop's pant legs hung a little lower than the other, always did, both cuffed, 'cause he had short legs. It was a dry still morning, no breeze, made me feel like this was the end of m'life. I felt sick and confused from the all night ride. My mouth and throat was dry, my head was pounding like a piston, and I was dizzy.

That's when she happened. The razor strap came down hard on m' heels, then the backs of m' legs. "Think you can run off whenever you feel like it. Mom like to have worried to death." Slap. And that is all Pop would say. Slap. Pop was furious, because he hadn't gotten any sleep from Mom worrying over every little noise outside. "Is that him?" And once again, "Listen, go look, see if that's him." Slap, goes the strap, and tears well up, can't help that, but I was too stubborn to let the tears go any further than the corner of m' eye.

I went through chores dreading going into the house and facing Mom. Her yelling always felt worse than the strap.

Months went by and clouds went rolling above without dumping rain. The corn was spindly. Not enough water and too much drying wind and dust.

It was hot all night, at least in the nineties, nobody could sleep. Even with my head by an open window, my skin stuck to the sheets and my hair lay damp on the pillow. Before the sun went down, the metal on the ole Model T Ford was hot enough to fry an egg. The heat shimmered and rose from the mounds of dust. Dust got in our lungs, piled against the fence rows, rolled across the Nebraska prairie for miles and miles.

The yard was dotted with a few weeds, drops of green that perked up the brown rust, the green of the weeds even looking pretty in the dappled shade of the oak tree. It grew just a man's length from the porch, its roots tangling with the board steps, making the steps rise higher on the right side. The rough boards of the porch floor leaned to the left, causing the porch to look more slanted than it was, with the steps leaning one way and the porch leaning the other.

"So what was the inside of the house like?" I wanted to know and was surprised at his memory for details. He had an extraordinary recall of images.

Well, inside, the wide plank floors was scrubbed daily but still looked dusty. Gray in the morning light. Mom was constant cleaning the house but even so it had a faint smell of rat. The mesh of the screen door was frayed. There was the peeling paint of the door frame.

I liked sitting on the porch, thinking of family inside and a world out there I'd get to. But it was hard to leave. The work and the house was like a cage with an open door. If someone had asked me why I didn't strike out on my own, I wouldn't have had an answer.

It was my job to tend to the animals. And the corn needed shucking if we was to hold on. Then, late fall, we'd have enough corn ready to take to Arapahoe. We'd come back with staples. Flour, sugar, coffee, salt, molasses. Maybe some print fabric Mom liked.

I had watched the supplies slip away, and, along with the rest of the family, felt the worry of hunger. We ate the gravy-laden bread. It was cheap to make with flour and lard. It would stay with ya longer than the naked bread. But on this one morning, I remember good smells come out of the house, the rough boards of the porch leading like a tongue directly into the kitchen, the boards mismatched on their meeting. The living room sat off to the side. Biscuits, light, perfect, with melted butter and molasses was waiting. Butter was scarce since we no longer had a milk cow. Molasses was too, but Mom often insisted on it, since it contained iron, and she believed it would make us strong. This was just part of her plan for all of us. She was the kind of woman who prayed solid and steady, beseeching God on our behalf, praying with the strength of a stone house.

The screen door snapped shut, with a creak and a bang, as I went inside, chores done, and sat down to breakfast. Breakfast meant a table set for eight, a table of thick boards laid out acrost two homemade sawhorses, places for my two brothers, Bob and Vic, and my three sisters, Roberta, Louella, and Wandah. Since my older brother Charlie left, me, Bob and Vic sat exactly across from each of the three sisters, with me opposite Roberta, Bob opposite Louella, and Vic opposite Wandah. Interesting how families sort out exactly where each member has to sit. Mom, or Ava Saylor before marrying Pop, and Pop, Clarence Grover Nolan, always sat at each end, as if they'd seen pictures of how families s'posed to look at mealtimes.

Mom sat straight and rigid, her dress pulled up to just below her knees. She shifted slightly to loosen its stretch across her lap and tugged down on it like she always done. The faded blue paisley swirled and emphasized her blue eyes. A few gray strands of hair poked out of her cotton headscarf that she almost always wore, and mingled with her brown hair. Pop was 'bout as thin as Mom was round. His worn khakis was always baggy and would've slid off without his black suspenders. His long underwear was unbuttoned part way down his chest, showin' his gray chest hairs. Mom always complaining that he ought'a button up.

And there was some joking and teasing, something Mom didn't much approve of, but even she had to smile when no one was looking.

"How come nobody ever hugs anybody around here?" Louella said this. She could come up with the darnedest things. At least that is what we often said.

Her sisters laughed a little. "Yeah, Ma, when was the last time you hugged us?" they asked with sarcasm.

"Oh, you're all rotten, that's what," Mom said. "You'd think you would all have more respect."

My sisters grew silent. Wandah and Roberta, petite, brown-haired and wiry at seven and nine, with Wandah the youngest, squirmed some in their seats. Louella, a bit heftier but also petite, and several years older than Wandah, slid her hands under her thighs and sat on 'em. Mom was in no mood to be toyed with. I grinned in her direction, careful like, ready to join in, then thought better of further stirring things up and concentrated on my plate.

Finished eating, I slid out of my place and went to feed the rabbits. There were four left, the other two eaten already. I looked into the cage and watched them eat the scraps of wilted lettuce from the kitchen garden. I was a little sad, thinking about how the larger one would probably be next for the supper table. The wooden slats of the cage blocked out their faces if I turned just right. That made me feel a little better. *Why, I can't be worrying over a silly rabbit.* Then I began to wonder if they would stay around if they weren't caged. I shook myself to get rid of the feeling of a dark cloud a'comin'.

Katie Nolan

7 Drink the Cup of Humiliation to the Dregs

Phrase for humiliation: 879,
Roget's Thesaurus, 1947.

1928, Bud, near Arapaho. I walked into the one-room schoolhouse,
situated about a mile from the old homestead. My army-green wool jacket
was unbuttoned because I'd gotten too warm during the walk. This was just
one day of many, although my attendance warn't good. Often, I had to stay
home and help with the harvest, or other farm chores. And on this day, like
so many others, I was late. I tried to slide into a desk in the back to avoid
Miss Kubick's gaze. Unfortunately, Miss Kubick looked up just then and
looked straight at me.

"Late again, Bud Nolan?" Her voice was severe.

"Yes, ma'am." I looked down at the inkwell hole, hunched up my
shoulders, and tried to disappear by shrinking lower into the desk.

"Well, open your book and do your lessons. Then, we'll have to go
about seeing the principal." Miss Kubick paused and looked right at me. A
school-marm look, and oh, my face turned beet red and become an even
deeper shade of crimson when I realized that Rebecca Smith was watching
and smiling at me. I tried to concentrate on lessons. But I was distracted by

40

the freckles across Rebecca's purty cheek bones and the fine, pale skin showing at the back of her neck. Finally, Rebecca bent her head down, her braids a
bit unruly because of her thick red hair, and began to read her text book.
Only then could I begin to put my mind to my lessons.

It was grammar: is, are, was, were; go, went, gone; who, whom.
All elaborated with examples: We will go to town today. We went to town
yesterday. We had gone to town last week. Actually, I always liked words, and
when the lesson turned to phonics I liked playin' with the sounds. I was on
my spelling lesson. E-lec-tric-ity. I played with it. E-lec-trick- ity. It made
me smile to myself as I mouthed the word, makin' it different. Arap-a-hoe.
Ah- rapped a hoe. Learn to spell the names of states: I-da-ho. I dunno. O-re-
gon. Oh-we gone? Cal-i-forn-ia. Calli' for ya? Californy. Callin' for ye. Miss
Kubick took that moment to sharpen her pencils and after three of them the
smell of pencil shavings took over the room. It mingled with the smell of
wood smoke from the pot belly stove that squat down in the back corner.

I still tried to concentrate but began to worry about the look on the
folks' faces that morning. It was pinched and they was silent. I preferred their
anger. Then, it all seemed to blur together, the folks, the smells, the wide
plank floors at my feet, the grammar and spelling lessons. I couldn't make
sense of any of it and I felt like I was surrounded by a gray haze, voices coming in as if from afar through the fog, me floating towards the opposite end of
a dim-lit tunnel. Folks sorta get lost in that kinda haze, a blur of confusion,
when there's too much goin' on and they can't think straight.

"All right, Clarence Raymond Nolan!" Fortunately, for my sake, very
early on I got the nickname of Bud and generally no longer had to put up
with the other kids making fun of my name. "Clare—rrr—ants, ants, ants,
ants in yer pants!" They'd shout it after me. Now, with Miss Kubick's emphasis on Clarence, the teasing is gonna start all over again.

Miss Kubick's voice penetrated my phonics reveries, and it made
all the students look up from their lessons. She pulled at her gray skirt and
carefully tucked in her starched white blouse, something I'd seen her do every
time she was getting ready for something. "You are going with me now to
see the principal." A few of the students snickered and she glared at 'em. Not
Rebecca. She glanced up sympathetic-like.

41

The principal, Mr. Birley, lived next door, one room of his home reserved for an office.

I, still blushing fiery red, followed Miss Kubick there. The heavy school door banged as we went out together. If only Rebecca hadn't seen me blush! Every time I saw Rebecca or sat near her my heart thumped wildly, and I just liked t' stay near her feeling this wild feeling.

I noticed on the path to Mr. Birley's house that the sky was full of dark clouds on the horizon, yet here, in the schoolyard, there were brightly lit ones overhead, waltzing their islands of blue. It was an early spring sky. I could smell that rain was coming.

Miss Kubick minced in front of me strutting like an old hen. I'd heard that she actually kinda liked us shoeless farm boys in tattered jeans, who sometimes smelt of barnyard, having just milked several cows and rushed off to school. Yet, she felt that to do us justice she had to teach us discipline. If not, we would never hold down a job, of that Miss Kubick was sure.

I knew the way to Mr. Birley's office. I was familiar with the steep stairs that led up to where Mr. Birley held court, a space made over into an official looking place from what had been a large upstairs bedroom in his old farmhouse. My legs felt watery and I felt dizzy. I didn't fear the paddle, honed carefully to sting the buttocks without leaving too much bruise. No. It was the humiliation. I felt deeply disgraced in Mr. Birley's office and then, again, when I returned to the classroom and the snickers. It was more misery than when I had broken my leg falling off the barn roof. Why, it was even worse than Pa's whippings with the razor strap. It was an occasion where I felt small, become an object of discipline, shrunk down in my own eyes. Set apart like a sick cow culled from the herd. Isolated.

In contrast to Miss Kubick's ambivalence, Mr. B had no doubts. Part of a wealthy family, he had not done well in business and felt the job of principal in this podunk place was beneath him. He had disdain for us all. Even for Miss Kubick, whom he knew had been a sharecropper's daughter down south before hard scrabbling through high school, working as a maid for folks like his to pay for room, board, and school supplies. No, he had little respect for us foul-smelling country folk. He longed to be back in the city with its raised sidewalks and neat lawns. The part of town where those who have jobs or own businesses that did not go under are doing just fine, thank you very much. The folks he had grown up around believed in Coolidge's remedies. Bail out the businesses and banks. That is what I had heard lots of folks around there say. And Mr. B often proclaimed this loudly. That day I was caught between Miss Kubick's duty to save me and Mr. B's disdain.

I swung around and grabbed Mr. B's paddle arm before the first blow. At first Mr. B looked startled, then a fury overtook him, his pupils dilated, his breathing quickened, like a predator coming in on its prey. But I had gotten older, my arms no longer those of a scrawny boy, rather, they were the muscled arms of a teen who'd worked hard on a farm. When Mr. B tried to grab my arms I wrestled free. But Mr. B would have none of it. He kicked me hard in the thigh, the way one kicks out at a snarling dog. I went down. Mr. B continued kicking me, outraged that I had taken his authority. I rolled to the side and managed to spring to my feet. Then, I planted my foot squarely onto Mr. B's rather ample backside, sending Mr. B tumbling down those stairs, with arms flailing upward, grabbing for and missing the stairwell rails.

Heart pounding, I ran past him and out the door and didn't stop for over a mile.

Nearing home, the reality of what I had just done began to sink in. *Damn.* I can't go home. Maybe they would jail me for assault, the way I'd heard they'd done to Jake Jasperson, one of the older boys that had knocked someone unconscious with a shovel in a fight at a dance. Or, they might send me to Boy's Reform School in Arapahoe, the way they had Paul Ward. No one ever heard of him again—he had been rejected by his family and not once spoken of—it was as if he'd died.

Now was the time to hit the road. They had hinted that maybe I ought to anyway, in a year or so, like my older brother Charlie.

I knew Mom had gone to the neighbor's to help out because they had taken sick. Pop had gone to town for wagon parts. I glanced around quickly to make sure no one else was there.

Mom had left a loaf of bread cooling on the window ledge, its smell floating in the kitchen, and I grabbed it. I also snatched the wool blanket off my mattress and rolled my second set of clothes in it. I scooped up two short lengths of rope off the porch, one to tie my bindle of blanket wrapped around bread and clothes, the other piece of rope, important as a spare, put into the roll-up next to my clothes. All else I'd need was in my pockets. A good knife, a fish hook and some string.

Within ten minutes I was on the road, striding purposefully, not looking back. A dark cloud had made it overhead and a few drops of spring rain come. Soft drops landed on mounds of dust and rolled off. Then, as quick as the cloud had formed, it dispersed and the sun was hot on my back.

I slowed to a steady pace. And maybe there was just a glimmer of hope that I could always return once things had blown over, the incident with the principal forgotten. I began to notice the surrounding pastures, the smell of rain on the dust, and the few birds chirruping their after-rain trills.

You know, like that song about the mockingbird? Tra-la-la twiddle dee dee, it gives me a thrill, to wake up in the mornin' to the mockingbird trill...

I watched as Dad got up and stretched, looked down at me with a mischievous grin and began singing off key as he headed out to the woodshed for more wood to stoke the stove. He knew that he sung badly and it was as if it amused him no end to subject whoever happened to be there to his light-hearted tunes sung with great gusto, especially on the choruses. "Tra-la-la, twiddle dee dee, it gives me a thrill..."

8 Cross Questions and Crooked Answers

Discord, conflict, also crow to pluck: 713,
Roget's Thesaurus, 1947.

August, 2009, Katie, near Glasgow Montana. Los Angleles to Glasgow is
a loop-back trip that covers a run from the west coast, across Arizona, New
Mexico and that little southwest portion of Colorado, then on through
Kansas, Missouri, and on into Chicago. From Chicago, I looped back west,
taking the northern route because I wanted to see Glacier National Park.

A gray light falls over the green rolling hills at a distance. Puffs of
wind worry the bushes at the side of the tracks. The grayness seeps into my
consciousness and I tremble, first my hands, then a small tremor in my belly,
and a chill starts up between my shoulder blades. I try to pull myself away
from this cool sense of disequilibrium, and I cast about for a distraction. I
grab the Amtrak magazine, catching an edge of the cover on the net holder
and tearing a page. I smooth the torn and bent edge and flip the magazine
open to vacation packages. Here's one, $3,000 for a package tour via train,
then bus, to the Grand Canyon. It includes the river ride at the bottom of the
canyon. I stare at the glossy pictures.

Why do I feel so shaky? This question, which strikes fear in my heart,
has no answer, as yet. I think, as yet, because I must find an answer. *Must.*

Is the answer out there, somewhere in the wind tugging at the bushes? Or is it in these notebooks that carry the stories I grew up with? These family stories certainly had a strong impact, made me feel different from others. Or, maybe I'm not so different. Perhaps everyone is hiding something. They are just pretending that everything is fine.

*I am still devastated by my writing mentor's feedback. She used the word dissociation after reading the first few chapters. And I cringed when another writer said: "I would want to stay as far away from that woman as possible (of course, she didn't know **that woman** was me)." I had to look up the word dissociation, and it is a mental health term that means that instead of being there for an experience the individual is like an observer of her own life. I have read of this in memoirs of childhood sexual abuse. An image of the child huddled against the ceiling during the terrible violation of her body, a sort of out of body experience. But I was never sexually abused as a child. Horrifying sexual experiences as an adult, yes, but not as a child. With some relief I read that it is normal to have some dissociation after a traumatic experience. But where is the line drawn? What is normal? Am I not normal? Isn't it common to feel like an observer of your life rather than being immersed in it? Surely, I have not had that much trauma? However, I fit the description in this: There are huge parts of my childhood that are blank. I've little to no memory of whole decades. And this is not just due to my age. I have never been able to remember much of my childhood.*

The train is slowing to a stop so I look up. They are waiting for a freight to pass. It rushes by, seemingly within inches of the passenger train windows, giving us riders the vertiginous feeling that we are being thrown backwards in movement, even though we are not. We are soon on our way and I turn to my writing.

I wish I had taken more notes in Mickey's writing class at Hugo House. I search through the ones I have, dropping the pages in the narrow space between the reclining seats. I have to contort my body sideways and use my feet to retrieve the sheets of paper. I lean back in the seat and read the first note in my journal, with the heading: *What's at stake? Where's the conflict? Why are you writing this section?* The latter question relates to what I'd written about my father's leaving home for the first time. He'd always grinned widely when he'd mentioned that he'd kicked the principal down the stairs and that was why he went on the road. But why am I writing about it? That question keeps coming up, a favorite of my writing teacher, it seems.

Well, why indeed? I don't always know, except the question agitates me every time she asks it. When I try to answer the question, I get a little stab of pain in my chest. A sense I'd like to roll on the ground a' sorrowin', as my parents would put it. I even feel angry! But that is unreasonable, I counsel myself. And I do what I have always done in the face of unmanageable emotion. I fidget and I smile. Mickey just doesn't see the connection between my father's story and my failed relationships.

My writing teacher is relentless in asking the question, "Where's the conflict in this scene?"

Conflict frightens me, I want to tell Mickey but I don't. I just cannot tell her about hiding in the forest as a child to avoid conflict (and my mother with her quickness of temper and whippings, and all the chores she had lined up for me).

I am not sure why none of these tales from the past seem to lead to conflict, at least the kind of emotional conflict Mickey finds interesting.

Except, I vividly recall one of Mickey's writing workshops. I had begun reading a portion of my father's story to the group of four other writers, thinking, now he had conflict! When I finished reading the section, the woman sitting on the couch beside me leaned over and whispered: "Did your father really get thrown in jail, then fight his way out?"

"Yes," I whispered back. That felt strange. I had never told anyone about the incident, so I was worried about the group's response. And I hadn't told the group that it was autobiographical. My classmate simply guessed correctly.

"Have I succeeded in painting a sympathetic picture of the characters?" I asked the group anxiously, hoping my classmate would say nothing of her discovery to the group.

"Yes, definitely," answered one of the members. I was relieved.

"Well, what about the guard?" asked another member. "Did he hurt the guard?" My stomach lurched, my hands began to shake, and my heart sped up. I had no answer for her. And I was not about to share what really happened. My god, what would they say if they knew he had killed the guard? I was saved by an interruption from Mickey.

"But why are you writing his story?" Mickey challenges. I am always fascinated listening to her because she is my opposite in appearance, beautiful, blonde, striking, petite. Well, I have the petite part... She has been a dancer. Also, a playwright with some of her plays performed off-Broadway. For me, all of this left a very romantic image. New York!

Sometimes when she asks, "What is at stake?" I am thinking, isn't it obvious? Then, I realize, with a sinking feeling, she is right. I am not sure what's at stake in writing my father's story.

I used to think it was my father's life that was at stake—and all the men's lives who have been threatened by police and incarcerated unjustly. My father had told me all the ways a guy could be put behind bars: "If ya had less than a dollar in yer pocket they vagged ya. If ya abandoned the sheep when you was herding. If they thought you was with the Wobblies. If they didn't like the looks of ya." My father's life was at stake, right? But this didn't seem to be obvious to my writing group. And my writing teacher says that she just doesn't buy it.

Why am I telling my father's story? Argh. After all that training in women's studies and feminist philosophy, shouldn't I be writing my mother's story? I straighten the curtain on the train window to symmetry, adjusting the tie backs so I can more easily see out, not really seeing the landscape, restless, wanting to get up and walk, do anything but continue writing.

My back aches from hunching over. I am chilled from the air conditioning, blowing from the vents. I search about in my backpack for my sweatshirt.

I think about the emotional stakes and cannot come up with a thing, except the lyric from a song in the play made into a movie, "Chorus Line," which goes: "I reach right down to the bottom of my soul and I feel nothing, nothing, nothing."

Maybe I can write my way to conflict, except my computer is in the overhead, and I don't want to bother my seatmate on the aisle to get up and get it. Fine. Use the notebook and pen. Sometimes it helps to just write longhand for awhile. Wait. Come on. It is what you learned in therapy. You are always afraid of bothering someone, when it is really about "bothering" your mother, who punished you when you got in her way.

Mom was busy. As mentioned, I don't actually remember too much of my childhood, but my mother told me that she didn't have time to read to me. She had to prop my bottle. I can imagine, because she had three babies, each two years apart, which meant when I was born she also had a two-year-old and a four-year-old.

I shrink further into the seat. Ask her for god's sake. What's she gonna say? No, I won't get up and let you out? I lean forward in the seat, hoping that my seatmate will get the hint. Nothing. I drag out my notebook and pen and put the seat tray down. The empty page. I doodle stick figures and stark outlines of trees and mountains. The outcome is similar to the outlined picture I made in fifth grade by tracing a picture with a piece of wax on a white ceramic plate and holding a candle there until the smoke blackened the plate around the wax tracings. I try a word exercise. Objects in one column and adjectives in another. No. Try verbs instead. Hemingway liked verbs. Action. Don't bore the reader with too much description. I fidget. I glance toward my seatmate again, who is concentrating on her reading, oblivious to my squirming in the seat. If I had the courage I would ask her what's at stake in that book she's reading. Ha. It's *My Antonia*. That book certainly doesn't follow Mickey's ideas of stakes. What's at stake, indeed! So there, Mickey!

Finally, "Excuse me, may I?" and I gesture towards the aisle. "Sure," and she quickly puts down her book and rises to let me pass. I squeeze by, but I don't get my computer down. I head for the snack car. I am suddenly hungry.

I walk slowly down the aisle, noting the snack bar sign with an arrow as I pass between the rocking cars. The cars on the Empire Builder are reassuringly arranged, similarly to those on the Coast Starlight. I only vaguely remember the transfer in Portland. Odd how lost I feel from the long runs between stations. Glancing out the train window, often feeling uncertain where I've gotten to.

I go down the curved flight of stairs, narrow enough that my elbows brush the walls.

As soon as I turn the corner after the last step, I am face to face with the menu on the wall. I read it without really seeing it at first. I am still unsettled with no identification of what is causing it.

I start feeling better as I find something I really like. A creamy macaroni and cheese that will be microwaved until nice and hot, advertised as "better than your mother's." It is my favorite aunt's mac n' cheese that I remember. How Aunt Roberta did not use a box but began with a bubbling cheese sauce in one of her giant iron skillets. How her kitchen chair wobbled on the uneven linoleum and when she saw me rocking in the chair, my feet wrapped on the wrung, she laughed and patted me on the shoulder. She was always smiling or laughing. I can still see her face tipped back, her eyes half-closed, her face crinkled in merriment.

I get a Perrier mineral water to go with it. Then, two chocolate chip cookies, their faint smell drifting through the cellophane wrapping, and a carton of milk for later. Ah, luxury.

I sit down at the little booth in the snack car and dig into the mac n' cheese, trying to avoid the repaired tear in the orange upholstery which pokes at the back of my leg. I look forward to taking the cookies and milk to the lounge car afterwards and savoring them slowly. For the moment, the question, What's at stake? is filed away, not completely forgotten, obviously, but perhaps I can bury it somewhere, where it won't continually disturb me.

9 Pretty Kettle of Fish

Absence or want of order: 59,
Roget's Thesaurus, 1947.

Done eating and returned to my seat, I continue to struggle to put down the stories my father told me, typing on the swaying seat-back tray, glancing up now and then, but all I can see when I look forward is the upholstered seat just ahead. To the left pinpoints of light march down the aisle just as they do on a plane. The aisle is incongruous because we clatter along through the night like an old-fashioned stagecoach, as if modern flight had never been invented. I open my journal: *At his first hobo camp he stole a chicken. He did some sheep herding. Almost froze to death. "So sheep herding, that's how I managed to settle in for awhile, get steady meals."*

1928, Bud, Lincoln, Nebraska. I came into the Lincoln jungle, believing in folks—not sure why—but believing just the same.

Maybe it was because my parents had taught me not to be too critical of others. "Ain't nobody better'n anybody else," they'd often say. And "You cain't never tell a hawk from a handsaw."

"What on earth does 'you can't tell a hawk from a handsaw' mean?" I interrupted.

"Well, I reckon it means that since you cain't tell, you ought not to judge." Dad stoked the fire.

"Oh, I should have gotten that. Sorry to stop the story. That your first hobo camp?" I stood up and warmed my hands over the wood stove.

Dad stood with his back to the stove. "Yep. And I got to be an expert."

I adjusted my pants as I came down the path, grasping the waist firmly, because the pants had a tendency to slip down when the rope belt loosened. My face was clean, never been shaved 'cause I was only thirteen.

I hadn't eaten all day and the hobos in Lincoln took me in. Later, I kept saying with amazement, "that was the best meal I ever had, 'cept for home."

I thought about my brothers and sisters, my mother and father, and wondered what they'd be thinking. They most likely would be worried, especially Mom, as she was the caretaker of the family. Oh, Pop did his part but he was not inclined to worry over everything. He was a man of action. I remember helping him load up the old Model T with rum, then parking it in a hay field where we covered over the entire vehicle with straw. When it was so dark you could barely see your hand outstretched in front of you, I watched Pop slip out across the field, disappearing within minutes. I heard the Model T crank up and saw its shadow burst out from the straw. I crouched next to the outhouse, its sour aroma mingling with the smell of dry hay, watching. And my heart started thumping when I saw the agents head down the road after Pop. He never got caught but Pop had other problems. Drinking, for one. As my sister Roberta, long after we all had left home, liked to put it, "He seems to like his liquor a little too much, a bit of the Irish, and Mom ain't very happy about it." Then, she'd always laugh some.

To outsiders it appeared that my parents had abandoned me. But I warn't abandoned—it was just that they couldn't feed everyone, so even if things could'a been worked out with the principal, I couldn't go back. I had taken in the message from my folks, too, when they had told my brother Charlie that "maybe he ought to hit the road so they could feed the rest."

I'd been taught to make the best of a bad situation. At that time, no one could've predicted how bad it was gonna get. In less than a year the stock market crashed, the crash of '29. When that happened, the faint hope of returning home was gone.

I settled into the camp. Still, a guy felt a little lonely sometimes.

"Hey, kid. Come over here. We gotta job for ya." I looked up and saw what I thought to be an old man, about fifty, sitting on an upside down wooden dynamite box, long since emptied of its contents. "Yeah, over here."

"What's the job?" I asked, feeling game for anything—no use brooding about family, what ain't possible no more.

"We need the fastest one here to go over to that chicken house and bring back one fer supper. You gotta be quick and slip in there and be down the path before their dog gets wind of ya." John had an air of authority about him 'cause he held down the jungle. He didn't ride the rails much any longer, being a little too old to keep up, and stayed at camp, sort of ran things. "Bet you can't outrun that dog." John's sun-darkened face was gnarled, arms deeply tanned, and his grin showed the wrinkles around his eyes.

"Sure, I can." I had taken a watermelon or two from neighbors' pastures back home. Used my bike to get away. It ain't bad to nab a chicken when there's a lot of us goin' hungry. That farmer won't hardly miss one chicken.

I left the hollow that cradled the hobo jungle by the river, noticing a few pots hanging in the willow tree as I scrambled back up the bank. A squirrel chattered in the cottonwoods, probably upset by the calico cat that often slipped through the camp looking for scraps. I'd seen the chicken house when I'd glanced back on my way down the slope, so I knew right where it was. The hard thing would be to avoid riling the dog. I could grab the chicken and tuck it into my coat, button down tight, and the hen wouldn't be able to flap loose.

When I got close to the coop, I looked around for the dog. It was nowhere in sight, so I pulled myself through the brush near the coop, using my elbows to drag myself along so's I was low enough to slip under the tangled thicket. The smell of the soil and the leaf mold tickled my nose and I was about to sneeze. Crinkling my nose and holding my breath, I drug myself on. Now through the brush, my face tickling from cobwebs, I was just three feet from a few brown hens pecking away at their feed. They weren't fenced in, which was gonna make it a lot easier.

I nabbed a chicken, feathers flying, and jammed it into my coat. I seen the dog snarling and coming after me. I took off running. I felt the dog bumping against the backs of my legs. He growled and nipped at my heels. The dog was faster than me. I was stumbling sideways, trying to run with the chicken under my coat. I was gonna be downed by the dog or shot by the farmer, for sure. My heart pumping. Then, I heard a sharp yip and thud. The dog had been chained and had come to the end of his tether. No one was at home. It was m'lucky day.

I entered the camp, proud as all get out, pulled that hen from inside my coat, squawking and twisting, and some of the feathers stuck to the wool. The rusty tin box that held wood was emptied and they told me to slip the chicken into it, then cover it with a piece of scrap plywood.

That evening I watched as the men in the camp plucked and dressed out the hen. First, the head was placed between two spikes on a chopping block. An axe dispatched it as clean as Marie Antoinette's guillotine, a few of the hobos joking that that's what they ought to do to the present politicians. The chicken flopped about while one of the men heated water over the fire. In the carcass went, then it was brought out by its neck, brown feathers dripping, steaming from the hot water. Now the pinfeathers would come out easy. Someone else gutted the chicken, tossing the steaming entrails to the camp dog, a big shepherd that gulped the mess from the worn grass in a few bites. The liver and heart were saved and went into the stew.

I was the guest of honor since I was the one who bagged the chicken, so no one asked me to help out with the meal. And they knew how to make one chicken stretch. Potatoes peeled and added. Carrots cut into small rounds with a pocket knife. Three large onions went in, chopped up fine. Someone offered some rice and that went in too. It expanded to the top of the dented, cooking pot, requisitioned from a dumpster at the back of a hospital.

A soft light fell across the camp as the sun began to lag towards the horizon on the opposite side of the river. When I sat down near the pot, dappled light came slant through the cottonwoods and did this little dance on everyone's sleeves. Battered tin plates with upturned sides were passed out, their edges glinting in the sun. One of the older men dished up the stew for eleven men, smiling at me as he gave me an extra half dipper. I adjusted the plate on my lap and dug in, the carrots sweet on my tongue.

"So, where ya headed, kid? Some of us are headed out to Colorado and some ain't."

"Colorado, I reckon." I said, but I really hadn't planned beyond getting to a camp.

"Okay. Well, eat hearty and sleep well. We gotta get up at four in the morning to catch the freight. Might be a rattler after that, but that's about it."

"What's a rattler?" I asked.

The men exchanged a knowing glance that said, "Kid don't know much, won't last long."

"A rattler is a passenger train. If you got balls you can ride inside, slipping into the restrooms when they take tickets. Or you can try the top." I slept soundly that night in the wool blanket from home. I hid back in the brush a ways and the low-hanging branches blocked the wind. I was also layered in two sets of clothes, easier to carry that way than in my bindle. The clothes and the blanket were warm enough, even when the temperature dropped that night.

I woke up to the sun filtering through the trees. My heart lurched. My surroundings was strange and I couldn't grasp where I was. Not remembering how I had come to be far away from home. I shut my eyes and tried to gather myself. The chicken. Okay. I remembered most everything about last night. I glanced out. Everyone was gone! My heart sank. I rolled over and pushed myself into action. Best way to deal with this feeling. Get busy. I pushed the fire of last night with the toe of my boot. Cold.

Focus on what you gotta do. Got this far. Gotta go on. I pushed and pushed myself to go into action. It felt like lead in my feet. Push. Push. Push. My body began to ache. A little dazed now, I managed to roll up my bindle and head for the trail to the train yard. That glimmer of hope that I might return home was more than gone now.

I travelled the rails, then, for several months, struggled to learn the ropes. Everyone offered advice. "Don't try to catch a rattler running too fast. You're likely to slip from the momentum and end up under the wheels, nothing left of ya. Stay alert, and stay hid all the time. The bulls will shoot at ya, especially if you ride the bumpers between cars. Walk over the ground you are later gonna run along to deck the train; this way you'll avoid running over a switch standard or some other obstacle. If you don't know your ground, you can end up an ugly, mangled mess. Nerve yourself 'cause there ain't no waiting to see which way the cat's gonna jump. You gotta screw your courage to the sticking place then take a leap."

I listened to them, all right, and, wanting to avoid the bumpers, tried riding the tops of trains. Occasionally, there was an empty boxcar on the freights, and I was able to lean up against a wall and catch some sleep. On the tops, no sleep there, because you had to cling to the swaying train, keep your balance, and watch for low-lying bridges that was so close to the train you might get yourself swept off.

10 Torment of Tantalus

Desire: 865,
Roget's Thesaurus, 1947.

I see one-third of a nation ill-housed, ill-clad, ill-nourished....If we can "boon-doggle" ourselves out of this depression, that word is going to be enshrined in the hearts of the American people for years to come.
—Franklin D. Roosevelt, 1882-1945, Thirty-second President of the USA

The fifth Nolan commandment, Thou shalt be a good judge of character.

1928, Bud, near Spokane, Washington, then heading to Glasgow, Montana. Quite some time after that first jungle in Nebraska, I was standing in the doorway of a boxcar, and holding onto the curved metal bar. I knew I was somewhere west of Spokane, heading toward Montana. The wind was warm, pleasant against the face, a soft, hair-rustling type of wind, and the lighting was the soft glow of dusk. No one shared this boxcar, and I relaxed and enjoyed the scenes rolling by. I'd just polished off the last stale hunk of bread in my bindle, and was making short work of a crisp apple I'd managed to grab from a front yard tree on the last stop. It was fall, nights cold, crisp mornings, warm days.

With each bite of apple I sighed, its burst of tart flavor more pleasant than 'bout anything I could remember. It took me somewhere, almost like I'd found myself, then like I was drifting away. It felt so strange I shook my head and breathed deeply, trying to make sure I was awake. Then I waited to take the next bite.

I looked up at the zigzag pattern of a hawk's wings. Those hawks would poise themselves over a mouse and swoop down to sate themselves, and, unlike us folks down here, they would exercise a hawk's calm. Up there, a house, a barn, and some outbuildings would look like small dots against the distant lit up hills. I saw the tin roof of a barn flashing a spray of light toward the sky. I imagined I was there in that house, just coming from the barn chores, then sitting down to supper.

All's I have to do, I thought, is find the next jungle and see about getting some work. With enough jobs in a row, I'll be able to save a down payment for a ranch. This thought was repeated so many times over the next long years it became like some of those verses to old hymns that we sung over and over. "Save up, settle down. Save up, settle down." You know, like that hymn, "Come Home," where the invite to get home just keeps goin'. "Ye who are weary come home, come home, come home..."

"Oh, yes, Dad, I remember that one. They were still singing it when I was growing up and Mom took us to the Ajlune Church of the Brethren. Usually sang it when there was a call to come up to the altar and be saved."

"That right. Well, it was around when I was growing up t'home too."

"But go on. I wanna hear more about riding in those boxcars." Dad looked up at the ceiling, then back at me, wiggled one ear then the other until I laughed and asked, "How do you do that?" Then, he cleared his throat and continued.

It was a long, slow sunset, streaking the wide horizon with the color of pink granite, like that on the floor of some old state capitol buildings. Those brushstrokes were mixed with pale orange. A sweet earth smell wafted up in the warm September evening. I breathed in the dusk air and knew contentment, then went to the back o' the boxcar and sat down.

My back against the cool metal, I watched the last of the sunset. Every now and then the whistle blew as the train passed through a small town, its back yards decorated with clotheslines and neatly stacked wood, pushed up under lean-to woodsheds. Being cold on the cars, coming through the mountains, coming to a whistle stop, then getting off to a warm gentle wind as the sun goes down on the prairie. That's pretty nigh heaven! I was a'glowing with the pleasure of it all.

58

Alone in the boxcar the night before, I had slept better than I had for days. It was always possible to get rolled and, in my last boxcar, I had been roused from sleep by someone grabbing for me.

"Hey, what you doing?" I'd shouted. It was a hobo with months of untrimmed beard and blackened hands and he wraps one hand around my forearm and put his foot against my chest. I went for the man's ankle and upended him. He went down. He was scrambling back towards me, and I could see the raised veins on his neck. He was swearing, "You son of a bitch. You son of a bitch." Just in time, I leapt to my feet, only to be brought down again when the desperate 'bo rolled into my ankles. Nothing was said as we rolled and grunted toward the open door. I could see the dirt as a blur, then, managed to push that old 'bo out the door.

Fortunately, for him, there was a soft mound of dirt all along the raised tracks, so's I saw the man get up stiffly from a cloud of dust. Many a man has been ground under a train by the sharp metal in just such a fight. So after this, I spent a few sleepless nights, my back pushed up into the corner of a boxcar.

It was a relief to ride one all night by myself. I had learnt to sleep in the rocking boxcars by doing the little exercise that one of the old 'bos had showed me. First, I'd say to myself, relax your toes. Followed by, work up to the ankles. Relax your calves, then thighs. Move on up to the gut. Keep going and by the time you get to your head, you'll be asleep.

Two men decked the train where I figgered I was, maybe, a hundred miles from Straw, Montana, a small berg with one general store, a wide porch stretching across its front, and, some folks didn't believe it, but it was the place I was born. I'd even been given a bad time about it, 'cause when I had answered the question about where I'd been born with, "I was born in Straw," I'd get back, "What's that, you was Jesus?" Then, everyone around me would laugh.

I grew tense at the sight of the men. I had had more than one run-in where I was purty near-death. I had learned that looking after details of face and clothes was part of figgerin' a guy out, whether they was out to roll ya. Both of the men wore shapeless caps, the bills crushed by the movement of their hands across 'em from using their caps for wiping the sweat off their faces. Each had on khaki pants thinned and limp from use, stained from work. Torn at the knees. One of the men had mended one knee, a crisscross mess of black thread around a patch of blue plaid flannel.

Their clothing smelled of smoke, likely from campfires in jungles, cooking meals in big pots. This odor mixed with the musty smell of the plywood floor in the boxcar, and reminded me of our old shed at home. Funny how smells take you back.

"Hey, kid, where 'ya headed?" The man with the patch spoke first. I smiled but I was cautious. "Chicago. Maybe Omaha. How 'bout you?"

"Don't have to be scared, kid. We ain't gonna bite. Just headed thereabouts ourselves. This here's my brother, Simon."

"Oh, I ain't worried," I said. "It's just that some people on the road take you for what 'ya got. Gotta be a little wary." I continued to look at them, not wavering from my gaze. That will let them know I ain't a rube, I figgered. And I was scared they'd turn me in, the way some guys did, when they come upon a kid run away from home.

I was a pretty good judge of character, had to be, to survive on the road. The patched knee was a good sign. The 'bo had learnt to mend, likely in some sort of domestic arrangement. Probably not someone who's part of the more criminal element, that generally seems lost to all family, no sign of having someone t'home.

"Well, we ain't like that. We're honest. Just lost our farm in Nebraska. Dried completely up. Nothing to do about it." This time Ben spoke.

"That right! Well my folks is still hanging on, out near Arapahoe. Ever been there?" Bud asked.

"Arapahoe? Why, yeah. We always went there to do our business. What side of Arapahoe your folks on?" Simon glanced at his brother, waiting for him to take over the conversation. He seemed reluctant-like to talk.

"North of there." They didn't seem like they were out to roll anyone.

"That right. Well, we was west. Maybe even ran into your folks, though, but wouldn't have knowed it. We always went into Arapahoe. But how'd you come to be on the rails, and looking like you done seen a ghost? Should have stayed on your folks' place if ya wanted steady meals."

"No. No. No. I ain't no runaway." I started shouting. Still scared they'd think I was a runaway. "Been on the road for several years," I lied. "That sound like I'm running scared?" I stared them down, squinted my eyes. They was silent so I went on, a little quieter:

"Anyways, we was goin' belly up. Not enough to go around. I was the second oldest and my older brother had already left. Figgered it was my time to go—they didn't need all those mouths to feed. My folks had told my brother Bob to head out too, so's there'd be enough to feed my brother Vic and the girls. The crop gone bad—the Dust Bowl hittin' Nebraska."

"Don't stay on the road too long, kid," Ben said. "It does something to a man. He begins to forget where he come from. Me and my brother ain't like that. We are saving up so's we can go out west and get a little land. Heard that there's plenty of water in the Northwest, so won't get blowed out."

"Well, that's what I'm gonna do!"

Nothing was gonna keep me from settling down. I knew I was gonna get a ranch of my own, no one telling me what to do, telling me to move on. No one looking at me the way someone looks at a mangy dog.

We all dozed a little, each in a corner of the boxcar. Ben was awake first and roused us.

"We're coming onto a little berg, kid. Don't ditch the train here. There's hostile bulls and you'll find yourself dead, or vagged and in jail."

I groaned. "Ain't had nothing for a day. Reckon I'm hankering after some food."

Hunger leaves ya less alert. Only with all your will can you stay tuned in to everything around. Sometimes hunger leaves a guy feeling angry. It'd be a low level of anger, but there ain't nothing to direct it towards. A man would frown, sometimes twisting his head this way and that, sticking his chin first on one shoulder then the other, trying to get hold of himself. Then, I'd remember my folks shouting at all of us: "We're hungry, too! It ain't gonna kill ya. Toughen up. We don't wanna hear how you're hungry—enough crying yourself blind—get to work or you'll be more than hungry." Good to get busy and try to ignore the gnawing feeling. Distract yourself somehow.

Simon and Ben looked at each other, then looked back my way. "Well, we've got an extra piece of bread. That'll hold ya until Omaha," Ben said. "I guess you know you gotta go through Chicago and double back west on a different track to get to Omaha."

I was grateful for the warning. I knew that they wouldn't tell me 'bout the bulls if it warn't true. I'd seen other men, many times, get roughed up with a whip, then hauled off to jail. I'd been vagged myself, several times, in for a night or two, a few welts on the thigh or back. "Thanks." I took their offering.

I ate the piece of bread slowly. I tore off little pieces of crust first. Each piece smaller than the length of my thumbnail. I measured this each time to make sure I didn't cheat. I knew if I didn't control myself, I'd wolf down the entire piece in two bites then suffer from hunger all night. If I disciplined m'self, I could make the piece last several hours, then hope that the hunger would be at bay long enough for me to sleep a few. It worked and I fell asleep with the bitterness of the sourdough lingering on m'tongue.

* * *

I came into Omaha around four in the afternoon, not sure how many days had passed, and headed for the nearest skid row, partin' ways with the two men, after thanking 'em for the company and the bread. I found a hotel, thinking I'd go to the restaurant kitchen, wash a few dishes for a meal, then head to a jungle for the night. No meal at the kitchen, but I made out okay at the jungle.

A few days later, I took a freight out of Denver, then hitched with truckers all the way up to Casper, Wyoming. I made my way through downtown Casper, and found the St. Claire Hotel. The lobby smelled of pipe tobacco and had worn plank floors. Purple velvet curtains, faded by the sun on the edges, were tied back on the one tall window by the front door. The desk appeared to be an afterthought, stuck in a far corner, dimly lit. I bypassed it, since no one was there and headed straight for the restaurant. I saw a couple of guys, looking to be fresh off the road, and sat at a table next to them. Both of 'em looked me over, leaving me feeling ill-at-ease.

62

11 Tender of Sheep

The economy or management of animals: 370,
Roget's Thesaurus, 1947.

The sixth Nolan commandment, Thou shalt never give up.

1928, Bud, Casper, Wyoming. "What you guys do? I see you're eating steady and at a hotel, too," I said, starting up a conversation, trying to see what they was up to.

"We're sheepherders, kid." They dived right back into their food. Sure didn't seem very friendly. I decided to try anyhow.

"How do I get in on it, then? 'Cause it sure looks good to be eating steady."

"Not everyone can do it," the smaller 'bo said, face deep brown and leathery from the sun and wind, now looking up and smiling, so I relaxed a little.

"What's yer name?"

"Bud. I think I can do it. We had a few sheep and I know how to bring a lamb..." I thought best to say no more lest they find out I didn't know a thing about sheep.

"Well, there's the boss. Let him know."

The boss sized me up for a few seconds, a short stooped man, wearing run-over-at- the-sides cowboy boots, and said, "Sure, we can use ya, kid. Have a meal with the guys and climb on the back of that truck when we take out for the ranch." I glanced out the hotel window and noticed that the truck was a wide flatbed with homemade railings on the sides and rough wooden benches lashed to the railings.

I settled in for the beef stew, breathing in its steamy smell, then stashing extra bread into my shirt pocket. I was glad, later, I had it, too, cause the trip to the ranch, clinging to the wooden bench, was long and cold. Wind blew off the Grand Tetons, bringing the chill of the dusted snow. The Wyoming prairies are endless leading up to the mountains and the fall wind had little to hold it back in between. The bunkhouse was an icebox and reeked of desertion after the fire went out, and the bunks was as hard as the bunks in the jails. Still, I hoped for steady work. This was a chance to start saving for my ranch.

"I'm gonna get my own spread someday," I said, trying to start up a conversation. "That's the only way a guy is gonna be free from all this."

"Sure, sure, kid. Just like us." And they all busted out laughing. I took it good-natured.

Early the next morning, the boss asked me a few questions, over a breakfast of a big bowl of oatmeal.

"Ever herded before?"

"Yeah, watched the sheep on my folks' place," I lied. I had herded cattle. How different could it be for sheep?

"Ever delivered a lamb?"

"Yep."

"All right. You'll do. But you know folks go crazy out there. We'll drop you off and you may not see nobody for six months. Sheepherders gotta have a heart of oak. You better figure out if you can take it now, 'cause it'll get you two years in the pen if you abandon the sheep."

"Okay. I reckon I can take it." I answered quickly, not wanting him to change his mind, and I knew if I willed it, I could take just about anything. After this short conversation, we loaded up the flat bed and headed out. Supplies included flour, sugar, lard, baking powder, a little jerky, some canned

64

goods. When we arrived at the sheepherders' wagon, an old- fashioned affair with wagon wheels grayed with time, and canvas stretched over some spines, we loaded the goods in.

"Whoa, don't drop the can a lard, kid. You're gonna need it bad."

I grinned, "Yep."

"You don't talk too much. You'll do just fine."

Dropped off with food, I began to look around. I had two sheep dogs to keep me company. They looked hungry so I made them some gravy, mixing the lard, flour, and water from the tank. I found the wood and got a good blaze going. Wagon with food stash, a cabin, and a fire for warmth. I smiled to myself, thinking about how this sure beats decking trains and skipping meals. I talked to the dogs. "Hey, what's yer name? Ya'll like it here? We're gonna be just fine now, just fine." Tails thumped and the dogs ate all the gravy.

I took off down a little trail, dogs following, and we located the sheep—1,000 sheep. I warn't used to that. The folks place had only twenty to thirty cattle. "Better get out and see what we got here, huh, Blackie!" Some sheep moved just above me and a few rocks clattered as they fell down a small ledge, the ledge rising from the short green grass, and looking like half of a cowboy hat sticking out from the hill.

That was the first day, then a routine took over. Pale gravy for the dogs. A little canned meat and corn for dinner, until the meat gave out. I supplemented it with a lamb, now and then, which I shared with the dogs. It was here I finally had time to think about the future. Save up and get my own ranch and family. But I'd often been so busy trying to deck the next train, get to the next job, avoid the bulls, look out after myself in case there was a thug on the boxcar—all of this sometimes kept my mind spinning so I couldn't really think.

There's gotta be things to do I hadn't thought of before. I began to wrack my brain, seeing if I could come up with better ideas. "If I just think hard enough..." And with that, I sat down on the thin mattress laid out on a wooden platform and stared at the wall of the cabin.

If I save my pay from herding I could buy a truck. I figger I better do that or I'll likely die if I keep on decking trains. Yeah, I could get from job to job without getting shot at.

65

Sleep in the back of the truck. Stretch a canvas so's it'd be dry. A truck could bring a lot of freedom.

My thoughts ranged over this better state of affairs for the entire first month, as I settled in for a long, cold winter.

* * *

"Now, what am I gonna do?" I was sitting near the door of the make-shift sheepherders' cabin and staring at the snow advancing against the single window, just to the right of the door. The door wouldn't budge. I sat frozen to the chair, as if the snow and ice had crept into my bones.

"I 'spose I might die this way. There's gotta be a way out. I'll go for it as soon as I figger it out. And after I get some rest. Outta wood—that ain't good. Guess won't be cooking the oats. Just as well eat some now. Will help me think."

I walked slowly over to the cupboard, the door long since burnt for warmth. "Ah, oats. Pretty good without cooking 'em. Eat and think about getting out of here." I was muttering half to myself, half to the dogs. I limped a little, partly from an old bicycle accident and also because I'd sat too long in the cold cabin.

Then, I let my mind go. Might as well think on the future. It ain't gonna get better worrying over things here. Just rest awhile. Wonder where my life is goin'. S'pose Pop and Mom didn't think much about how they was doing and they just kept on getting up and goin' about their business. I ain't gonna do that. Gotta think about what I'm doing or I'll end up like 'em, goin' nowheres, and worrying all the time, too. You'd think they'd not have to worry since they'd not really been shot at by the cops the way I was—well, maybe Pop was—he never talked about it—just disappeared for a few days and came back with some money—knew it was from running the rum over to Wyomie. How come he'd keep on? Mom yelling at him and nothing changing. How could he stand it? He shouldn't of been strapping us that'ta way, though.

An uncomfortable knot of feeling rose up, hit my belly button—scared me. I began to doubt whether there was another soul that cared whether I was living or dead. Well, better do something so's to feel better—don't do no good to sit here feeling sorry for yourself—likely to end up dead that way, too. I pushed against sleep. "It ain't gonna work to get that door open—gotta break out the window," I said out loud to no one. I rose from the chair and began running, then laughing, when I saw that the dogs were running after me in crazy circle after circle, around the cabin.

My head cleared a little and I found a hammer and struck the glass hard with it and it fell, tinkling back onto my chest, falling down my pants onto my boots. I shook the glass off my clothes, avoiding the shards so as not to cut my hands. Then, I careful-like began to pick the glass away from the snow, pressed up against what was left of the window.

"This is gonna take awhile," I said, more to myself than the dogs, but Blackie looked up, head cocked to the side, while Boner looked away with indifference. "When I get outta this one, I ain't gonna come out here again, ain't worth it, not if I want to live to see my own ranch. No, ain't never gonna do this again." Vow after vow of what I'd never do again was sandwiched between each handful of snow that I pulled down into the nearby corner of the room. It froze in place, not even wetting the floor, and I looked at it in surprise when it didn't melt. "I'll tunnel out. It's gotta work—snow most likely will be drifted and a tunnel will get me some daylight."

On I worked, the kerosene lantern sputtering, reminding me I'd better hurry before it snuffed out. Just to reassure myself, I walked over to the fireplace and looked up the chimney and found that I could see a little shaft of light. "Okay, then—it ain't up higher'n the cabin. I'll make it outside and take a look see—gotta be a way to get to the wood outside and the supply wagon out back. Hmm...ought'a be proud of myself—don't panic, just like my Grandpa Nolan taught me—if you're in a pickle just relax, think, figger things out—there's always a way out. Reckon I might'a got my cussedness and cheeriness from him. Yep. Mom used to say Pop got it from him, so's I reckon I did too. Lucky, I reckon."

I worked hard at the tunnel, knowing from past experience that if I set myself a task and didn't give up, I'd rid myself of that inner ache, that pain below the heart—a pain that occasionally threatened to linger. Maybe this is the way it is—always getting pain—after awhile it never goes away—see why you wouldn't wanna live if it stayed there, weighing a feller down— gotta not stay around with that thought—that thought scared me—but I ain't inclined— enough people wanting me to die—no sense me thinking about it, too. Mom said it sometimes, that she wished all of us wasn't around, but I don't think she meant it. They'll throw me in prison for sure, if'n I don't get myself outta here and check on the sheep. Ain't fair—almost t' die and they only care about whether their sheep make it. I ain't gonna die. I ain't goin' to prison.

I shivered at the thought of prison. Think I'd rather die than be locked up somewheres. I made it through the first two feet in thirty minutes. Goin' like this, I'll make it out in less than two hours. With that thought, I cheered up, and even began enjoying the task, watching the tunnel get bigger and bigger.

"We're gonna make it, Blackie," I said, reassuring Blackie as if I'd never had any thoughts that we might not get out alive. "I'm gonna make it." I said this aloud, firmly, and Blackie looked up trustingly, and proffered one little thud of his tail against the floor. Boner had crawled under the bunk and peered out mournful-like. I patted Blackie's head. I shouted at the window, and at the little opening of the tunnel. "I'm gonna make it!"
Then, the lantern sputtered out, the last of the kerosene gone. I felt for the chair. All was pitch black.

Dad looked up at me after he'd finished and to lighten things up said, "Well, warn't that a purty kettle of fish." I was standing with my back to the stove.

"Phew," I said. "That certainly warn't easy." And noted how I always returned to my language within minutes after I settled in at home. Even in my thinking, because at that moment I mused: "That's 'bout as crazy as she gets. You was only fourteen." Sometimes, in my life as a professor, I practically feel schizophrenic because my thoughts are so different from the academic lingo I feel compelled to use. I was brought back to the moment as Dad continued his sheepherding story.

* * *

In the pitch black I was relieved by a thin slash of light in the fireplace. I stared at it for a minute, for reassurance. Now, there'd be more risk of cutting myself on a stray piece of glass. "Reckon ya don't need light to make a tunnel. Nope." I found a shirt by feeling my way to the bunk where one hung over the rail. I wrapped the shirt around my fist, then tore hard enough to get one sleeve off to wrap it around the other fist.

I continued working, grateful for the sound of Blackie's breath. Otherwise, the stillness from the blanket of snow over the cabin would have left me in silence 'cept for the sound of my own heart beating. The racket made from tossing the handfuls of snow was reassuring. "Ain't no need of feeling upset about no light. Dark is the same as light—just gotta remember that everything's the same. Besides, feeling upset about the dark is just how kids are—I ain't no kid—jeesus, Blackie, now don't brush against me so's I think you're a rat or something—jeesus it's dark in here—reckon it's dark when you die—I ain't gonna die—dark is the same as light—everything is just the same. The tunnel is big enough to crawl into, I think."

I extended my arm, propping my legs against the wall below the window so that my body could wriggle up into the tunnel. It was harder now because I had to ream out the tunnel so I could reach the snow back behind me as I went. Be crazy if I froze in some tunnel out a cabin window. Don't s'pose they'd find me 'til spring—saw animals that way—dead and exposed after the thaw.

A chunk of the tunnel caved and filled my mouth and eyes with snow. So the snow is looser out here. Probably get out of here in no time. Maybe it is better to crawl back into the cabin and take a rest—eat some more oats— that'll keep me goin'. Can't be too many more yards. Maybe pressing my feet up against the top will keep it from caving.

I worked for thirty minutes, pressing on each square foot of the top of the tunnel. Then, I worked another foot, then pressed the top again, first rolling onto my belly, then, rolling over and looking up, even though it was dark and I couldn't see anything, so my feet could feel the top. Looks like I learnt something from listening in on Grandpa and Pop's goin' on about how to survive this and that. Looks like I was one of the smart ones they talked about.

"Yep. I know what to do." Six feet out I felt the bottom give way and I rolled into the sunlight. I was right. The drift was deepest up against the cabin. By stretching myself out on the snow, I half crawled, half walked to the supplies wagon. If I was careful, I wouldn't break through the frozen crust. Using the same method, I rolled the wood and five-gallon can of beans back. This was my first trip. Next time out, I did the same thing with a small jug of kerosene.

Then, I worked the head of the tunnel so I could move back and forth, cabin to supplies wagon. I'll be all right if it don't snow again—well, even if it does, I'll be all right. It won't be bad to do it again—and now, I'll have some light. I crawled through the tunnel back into the cabin, tuckered out, and allowed myself to lay back on the floor for just a moment. I willed myself up and pulled down the blackened bean pot, got a fire going, and hung the pot over the fire. I cooked up the beans, then made gravy with the lard and flour, and shared that with Blackie and Boner, then, ate hearty myself.

"Tomorrow, we'll go out and check on things, eh, Blackie." With that we drifted off, caught in a scene from one of those Zane Grey novels Pop used to keep on his shelves. It was a dreamless sleep, in a landscape of drifted snow, cracking frozen branches, and a thin trail of smoke rising out the chimney.

I'd heard the stories in several ways, details varying slightly from time to time. And I knew about Dad's interest in Zane Grey novels. Grandpa Nolan had a large collection and would loan them out to us, so Dad would sometimes be reading one in his upholstered rocker in the tiny living room, carved out with a short wall where once there was none, as our home was originally a goat shed. When I was a child these stories made my father, former hobo become wildcat logger, seem bigger than life. Early on as a logger he had decided not to work the landing but to be a tree topper. A hundred feet or more, up he went, using rope and spiked boots. I believed he could do anything.

There is no image stronger in my childhood than that of myself as a skinny child with braids dashing out the door when I heard my father's pick-up truck come into the driveway. He was smiling, always smiling, and chuckled when he opened the door of the truck and saw me standing there. Ritually, he handed me his tin lunch box. A black, partially rusted box with a hooded top that graced wires to hold a thermos above the rest of the lunch. Sometimes these wires slipped and the thermos smashed the sandwiches down. They were always still eaten. My proud assistance freed his hands up to carry his power saw and his extra coat and rain slicker.

He parked by the shed, with its greasy floor from working on this or that old jalopy that barely ran. He kept the latest junk running by working weekends in there. The shed sat just beyond the clothesline. He would duck down to go under the line, avoiding brushing off his tin hat. Then, past the lilac bush that sat on the little rise leading up to the clothesline, around the back of the tar-paper shack where we lived, up through the woodshed, its smell of dust and cedar. Just to the back of this woodshed, the beginning of a fenced in pasture. Beyond the barbed wire fence, a pile of kitchen scraps, potato peelings, trimmed out rotten spots of carrots, beet tops, carrots and beets that had been left in the ground for winter and tunnelled through by worms. Now left out for the coyotes, or whatever critter got there first.

One hundred acres of pasture was the only thing that separated the woodshed, the shack and outbuildings, from thousands of acres of Weyerhauser timber, leading up to the jagged peaks of the Cascade mountains. These peaks included Mt. Rainier, which could be seen just a quarter mile down the road when one turned a sharp corner on the gravelled road. The road became impassable for days some winters.

I had repeatedly set out for Mt. St. Helens to the south, a lunch of bologna sandwiches, an apple, and some cheese tied in a big red hankie and fastened onto what I'd imagined as a hobo pole that I hoisted across my shoulders. Inevitably, I'd come up against a high rock bluff that seemed to extend miles in both directions, and I would have to turn back if I was going to make it home before dark.

My father's cheerfulness and approval sustained me, this shy child who had difficulty expressing herself, so much so that one relative or another would sometimes get in my face and shout, "Speak up, child!" Then, I would cringe away and my voice would get even softer. To spite them?

Sometimes my father would rescue me from conflict by saying in a firm, but quiet voice, "That's about enough." That would stop whatever cousin or sibling who happened to be pummelling me.

I began to avoid conflict by going into the nearby woods and hiding for hours, sometimes all day, crouched beneath a tree and holding as still as possible, waiting, and hoping that, if I held still long enough, animals would come up to me. I could smell the forest floor and feel the stream of filtered light, as if it had substance. More than once I felt bathed in this light, felt moments of pure bliss, as if held by welcoming arms; I did not want to leave the forest and go back to the house.

I don't want the memories.

* * *

My world on the train becomes pastel with anonymity, the opposite of belonging to a big family with mother, father, numerous aunts, uncles, cousins. I am surrounded by anonymity, an anxious and fearful feeling, completely disoriented, an aspect of travelling alone. There is the unknown landscape. The hum of indecipherable voices competes with the chug of the rails. An image of a face of a woman who has amnesia, a face twisted with confusion and terror, trying to figure out who she is. I think about returning to my old life in Seattle. Should I return? I try to find and cling to something familiar, knowable.

12 Fall Foul of the System

Contention, also come to the scratch, measure
swords, take up the cudgels: 720,
Roget's Thesaurus, 1947.

Our blue and white kitchen was flooded with early morning light from a clear summer sunrise. I was sitting with Dad by the stove.

"Were you ever depressed, Dad? I mean, times were pretty hard."

"Well, sometimes I felt like I'd fallen into a deep hole. Got tuckered out. But depressed on the road? Are you kiddin'? Ain't no time for poor folks to carry on thataway. But it was kinda hard to leave camp sometimes. I had begun to stay longer in hobo jungles, almost getting the job of caretaker. That scared me. I didn't wanna see myself dying, alone in a jungle, like some of the old 'bos I'd seen, disconnected from family, no one to get in touch. But, if I stopped moving, I figgered I'd die. I always managed to move on. Besides, not much choice, you know. You either fight back or lay down and die. That's why we went on the big march."

1930, Bud, Demonstration in Union Square, New York. As I got close to the camp, a regular Hooverville, I could smell the rank odor of kerosene-soaked oranges as they floated down the river. It reminded me of what Harry had said: "They'd rather see us starve and just replace us when we conk, than give us a dime more of pay, or let us have a scrap of food, food

73

that they are ruining with kerosene and throwing away to hold prices up." I had hard-travelled for days to get back across the U.S. from Los Angeles to New York, following Harry's clues as to where he was going. All the hobos used symbols painted onto water towers or fences, to communicate where it was and warn't safe to go, where they had gone.

As luck would have it, Harry was in New York to organize for the Wobblies, and he'd left that message for me on a Chicago fence near the yard—a national day of protest was planned for March 6th, demanding relief and unemployment insurance. As I entered the camp, I heard Harry shouting after me: "All hail! Let's roast an ox!"

I just grinned and grinned, then shouted back: "Forget the halloa before we're out of the woods, you old 'bo!" We did the usual greeting—a few socks on the arm, more shouting.

I wrapped the top half of the canvas that covered our shelter for the night with rope, and tied it into a sailor's knot to the right of the doorway, its loose end dangling and bouncing in the wind. A frayed army blanket hung in the doorway and the bottom end was anchored with a large stone to one side. It smelled faintly of cat piss where one of the camp toms had gone by and marked. Our bindles were tossed towards the back, out of easy reach. Since this was a semi-permanent camp, some of the structures were made up of bits of scrap lumber nailed together and topped with used corrugated tin, then covered over with canvas. Newspaper had been scrounged and crushed into the cracks between the boards on the sides, causing the shanties to smell of molding paper. That smell mingled with the faint odor of urine, not helped by the warm sun.

Water buckets sat every few structures and were filled from the river nearby. Anytime someone had a need for water to bathe off the stink of their job it was available. The camp also used the water for washing dishes. A thin skin of ice sat on one of the buckets, the temperature dropped below freezing the night before. The camp was in an uproar, and not only due to its barely hanging together under the blustery weather, odds and bits of canvas and board bouncing in the wind. It was tense with the excitement of the planned march the following day. The agitation rose between those who supported the march and those who didn't.

"Well, look, things aren't going to get better of themselves. We don't stand to ever get out of this," and he gestured down the row of structures, "unless we do something. We've got to get out there and let folks know what is going on." Harry was speaking, surrounded by men, women and children from the camp.

I listened to Harry and the other folks. I hadn't been on a march before and wasn't sure whether I was gonna join.

"A big showing will put pressure on the politicians. If we don't put pressure on them, it is business as usual. They are just as happy to continue on as they have been doing, and none of them are living like this. And the bosses aren't either. Do you think Mr. Armour himself is worried about any of you? No, he is in bed with the politicians and they are both happy to make gains at your expense."

It made sense to me. So, when Harry asked who was ready to join the Union Square march, I was there, saying, "I reckon I'll go with ya."

"You're just gonna get yourselves beat," one of the men stated, shaking his head. "And nothing will come of it," from another.

"Yeah," another joined in. "When did marching down a street accomplish anything? They will be just too happy to club you or shoot you. Why, they are probably hoping that you are foolhardy enough to go down that street."

"You might be right," one of the quieter men said, "But even if the odds are against us, what other way do we have of fighting back? We can't get up an army and fight them. And we can't ask politely and get results. You know where voting's gotten us. So, what else do you suppose we could do?" There was a pause of silence.

"That sounds about right to me," I agreed.

The men were coming 'round. They could see the logic in what the man they had dubbed "the quiet one" had said. They knew what they were up against. And they weren't willing to sit and do nothing. The whole camp, with the exception of a few of the older men and designated women, was going to Union Square. That night, me and Harry stayed up late, adrenaline pumping.

"Hey, you need to think about what you're doing on the road," Harry said, needling me some.

"I am thinking!"

"Well, yeah, that's not what I mean. I mean, why don't you join the Wobblies? Life doesn't mean much if you're just a schmuck trying to get by. Need to go for something bigger than yourself, or someday, you'll look back and see how hollow it's been. Just lived the span, nothing more."

I frowned, looked down. It irritated me when Harry went on about joining up with him. I wasn't sure why, but I knew that I didn't trust it. Just can't do it. For a moment I was at a loss for how to get Harry on to something else. Then, I thought of something.

"Well, I learned the hard way that joining up with others gets ugly. Soon as you think you trust some guys, they do something that would send 'em to hell, and you with 'em. You know there's lots of that type out there. It's okay to have a few friends, sure, but a group... I just ain't gonna join up with something."

"You need to trust something, Bud, besides a friend or two, because those friends won't be there forever, but, as long as you are alive, you have to live with what you've done with your span. And it won't mean much, when all is said and done, if you haven't hooked up with something that means something."

I knew well that was what drove Harry. His organizing. His belief that things could be better. But I just ain't gonna be able... And I was more out of sorts by this talk than made sense. I'd disagreed with Harry before, so why did I feel like I was losing control, like a guy coming off a bender? I admired what Harry did. Why couldn't I see myself joining up?

I got up from my crouch on my bindle in the tent and stretched, turning away from Harry. "Reckon we ought to get some sleep. Big day..." I headed out, flipping the blanket back over the top of the shelter. Went to splash water on my face.

Later Harry told me all about how he figgered I had trouble trusting folks, like him, and how that can leave ya isolated, never sharing what's on yer mind, getting just too damned independent. I told him I thought he was full of shit and Harry just let out a sharp breath.

As we entered Union Square, my heart beating like a drum, I was caught up, along with over 100,000 other workers, in the excitement.

Looking up, I saw machine guns mounted on the roofs. I glanced down quickly so as not to lose sight of Harry. I heard a voice booming from the speakers' stand.

"Mayor Walker has prohibited our march. Police Commissioner Whalen has threatened to break it up with force, and he has refused us a parade permit. This is in spite of the fact that many capitalist organizations, including, recently, the Queen of Roumania, have been allowed to parade freely." A pause and a strange silence fell over the massive crowd. It was a moment of tension. It was William Z. Foster speaking, the second time I'd heard him from a stand.

"Shall we march in spite of Whalen and his police?" Foster's question was followed by more tension that flowed through the crowd in murmurs. Then, me and Harry shout with tens of thousands of workers, "Let's march!" William Z. Foster gave the signal to start and the procession began to move down Broadway.

But before we had hardly begun, mounted police charged through the crowd. Police on foot, clubbing in every direction. I ducked the baton of the mounted cop, only to get it from the back by a cop on foot. I felt the club's contact with my back—grateful he missed my kidneys where he was aiming.

Harry motioned to me, barely able to move to the right or left from the jostling of the crowd. Harry shouted "Down this way!" Then, his voice was drowned out in the commotion. I saw him turn and followed him down the adjoining street. There, the relief was short lived. I saw them grab for Harry. Then, clinging to Harry's jacket, I tried to jerk him free, but in the scuffle both of us were knocked to the ground and cuffed. We were among the few workers who were arrested—the cops having planned to club the rest out of the Square.

The cops drug me up first, twisting my cuffed arms up behind my back, then shoving me, stumbling, down the street and into the open doors of a paddy wagon. Harry wasn't far behind. We found ourselves facing two men, one black, one white, on the opposite bench. Names were exchanged. "This is Joe. I'm Matt," the black guy said. "We're part of the organizing committee." Still in the flush of the success of gathering so many unemployed together, Joe and Matt spoke full of fire. It was actually unfortunate for me and Harry that we'd been taken in with part of the committee. Because of that, we were looked at with more suspicion and eventually Harry was identified as "that damned I.W.W. Red." Shoved into a cell with the two men we were brought in with, we sat on the wooden bench, awaiting our fate.

"Damn, Harry. You sure know how to get us in a fix," I said, grinning a little. I admired Harry's courage and had begun to believe in some of what Harry had been saying all along.

"Well, you didn't do so bad yourself." He turned to the other two men. "Anybody out there going to try to get you guys out? Somebody from your party?"

"I know they'll try," Joe says, with confidence. Matt said nothing, looking grim. Harry glanced my way and tried to make light of the situation.

"Looks like we went up like a rocket and are a'comin' down like a stick."

"Well, that stick's still aglow, ain't it," I said. We kept up the banter, trying to keep ourselves from feeling all was going to wrack and ruin. Just as soon as you'd be close to something, it would slip through your fingers. It was those thoughts we worked hard to keep away.

For three days we were held without charges and without bail. Then, someone from the Communist Party Committee managed to get news in to their two men. "The press is going wild, blaming us for everything. A cop has been seriously injured and they have threatened all of you with the charge of murder if he dies."

Each report coming in made us worry more. The committee fought for a jury trial, knowing the country was beginning to have sympathy for the unemployed. It was denied. All four of us were brought before a judge and heard the verdict. "Six months in the New York County Penitentiary." The cop had not died. If he had, we all would'a hung. So much for luck that ain't luck.

All four of us were shuttled out the door and headed to the county pen. Once there, we were separated. "Cause we was dangerous reds," they said. The first day, I woke up in a four by six cell. Later, read it was four by six and one-half foot exactly, but I made a purty good guess. A bunk on one side. Barely room to walk. No plumbing, just a bucket in the cell to relieve yourself. The stench from buckets in every cell down the line was sickening, about as bad as when I'd stirred up the foot-deep floor of our old chicken coop. I rose to sitting and was facing heavy steel doors. I shook in the morning cold, because of the thin jail suit. I worried about Harry.

Landed in a tomb, I was, and I willed myself not to think about the fix I was in. Would I ever see Harry again?

Unknown to me at the time, I had entered prison on a day when the weekly bathing cycle was in process. I was roused from my sense of doom by a voice shouting, "Bath!"

A guard turned a key and my door clicked open and flung wide. I followed the rush of men toward the showers. For who knows what reason, three men at a time were only allowed five minutes from the time the first man entered until the last man was out. The men were in a frenzied rush to undress, wet themselves, grab clean clothes, dress, and rush out. I saw the slower man in front of me get a shove and a violent kick in the behind. I managed to keep up with the rest and put on the too long pants thrown at me.

I spent the rest of the day in my cell, barely able to walk or stand in it, then went through another rush to the mess hall. Because of grubs in the food, the men at my table wretched and didn't eat. Passing a matchbox from man to man, we collected the grubs. As we went through this little resistance, the black man, Matt, the fellow I'd been brought in with, raised his hand signalling that he wished to go to the bathroom. The guard nearby ignored him. Matt signalled again, in obvious distress. The guard still studiously ignored him. Then, we were all marched out of the hall, and that same guard drug Matt back, and cursing and beating him, made him clean his spot. For this "prison infraction" Matt was given five days in isolation on bread and water. I knew about this type of discipline, the kind that makes you feel like as if you was chewing nails, and began to go numb in the face of spending the next six months in jail.

Days went by, and I became known as Smiley to a few of the men. Fortunately, most of the prisoners generally kept their distance, so I didn't have to fend off the roving gangs who had free rein in the place, plying their drug trade of marijuana, heroin, and booze, selling the fresh young ones into sex slavery.

I did join the men in complaining about Connolly. None of us could believe the pull of that guy, the former president of the Borough of Queens. "Jeez. He steals millions and gets privileges, while we steal a cow and get a stinky cell and rotten food." One of the men started the conversation at the table where I was playing cribbage with the man across from him.

"Yeah, even his capitalist friends couldn't save him, he was so wild, taking the city's money as if he had a right to it." I nodded at this, as my cribbage partner spoke.

I joined in. "Yeah, I seen him strolling 'round the grounds with the guards like he owned the place. Why, he even was out there practicing at the rifle range with 'em."

"Damn, that man lives in the hospital, takes up a bed even if some other poor sucker needs it. They eat high on the hog in there. Fresh fruit and vegetables, even ice cream!"

"Something we ain't gonna see." This came from the man at the adjoining table where they were playing poker. I nodded in agreement. We all went back to concentrating on our cribbage or cards, some guys shaking their heads.

That night, in the cell just below mine, the guy got sick, appendix, I heard later. I could hear him groaning. "Hey, you okay?" I called out, but there was no answer. Now, everyone was awake and there was lots of calling out.

"Hey, Smiley, that you?" Someone yelled out from above.

"Nope, guy below me."

"Oh. Sounds bad."

I lay on my bunk wide awake. Occasionally I dozed off, but, when the groans got louder, I jerked awake. A man got no control over things in here, even to help another guy out. At least out there I had some fresh air and could run from the cops. Here, we're sitting ducks. And what if I get sick? I can't get sick. If a guy does in here he ain't likely to make it out.

I tried to distract myself by wiggling my toes and fingers. Then, I practiced wiggling my ears, first together, then one ear at a time. Yep, they all still work. I brought my knees to my chest and it relieved the pain in my back. Then, I rolled out of bed and began jumping jacks, leaping higher and higher, palming the ceiling with its orange-stained plaster, and avoiding the bare light bulb as I slapped at the plaster.

Twelve hours later, I heard the guards come. They jerked the man up as he cried out in pain, and I folded myself into a tight roll, goddamn sadists! The man was forced to walk the hundred yards to the hospital. I never knew whether he survived or not. If he didn't I knew the body would be dumped on a ship, along with a pile of other bodies, carried down the East River, and buried in Potter's field.

The next afternoon, I played cards with the other men, kept my thoughts to myself, and listened carefully to their exploits. It was as if the subject of the man's suffering during the night was taboo. I began to fear for myself. Is this my future? A long, slow life in and out of prison? Die alone in here? I lay on my bunk nights, worrying.

* * *

It had been four months when I was brought before the parole board. Much to my surprise I was let out early. What I didn't know at the time was that Harry had used his connections and had been able to get himself out, then work on getting me out.

I left the prison yard with a stiff new pair of shoes, bad-fit clothing (pants legs always too long), and nothing more. No apology from them. Nope. Just a statement. "You are free to go. The charges are dropped."

I saw the headline later. UNION SQUARE MARCH INCREASES SYMPATHY FOR THE PLIGHT OF WORKERS. Now, the government was gonna get serious about unemployment insurance. Of course, besides the march, they might've been pushed by some of the armed marches. Masses of us, marching down the street with rifles thrown over our shoulders, must've shook 'em a little.

I was back on the road. I knew I had to get rid of the prison duds or I wouldn't get work. I lifted a pair of pants from a clothesline and a pair of boots off the back porch. I got my first job in a railroad grading camp. Lucky, this one paid. Once I had a decent stake, I drug up and headed out on a freight, hoping to find Harry, knowing I had to figure out what I was gonna do to settle down.

2009, Katie, north of Seattle. Passing through Everett, I wonder if Dad knew about the Everett Massacre. I learned a little about that, along with the workers' struggle, when I was a sophomore in high school. We spent a few days studying the Great Depression. When our history teacher, Mr. Taylor, began talking about the Depression and how that created migrant families and migrant workers, I perked up and began to listen. Generally, I had a bad habit of staring out the windows, daydreaming, but that day he really got my attention. He began asking students if their parents had talked about the Depression and my heart was pounding for fear he would ask me.

His voice came through faint, and as if from a radio with static, making it difficult for me to focus. "How about you, Katie, do you recall anything that your parents said about the Depression?"

"My Grandma and Grandpa Nolan had to flee the dust bowl."

"What about your Dad? What happened to him when they had to migrate?"

Heart pounding because I knew I was about to lie, I frantically searched for something to say. "Well, it wasn't so bad for my Dad. He got a job on a dairy and stuck it out. At least until he married my mother, that's what he did." My face was beet red. Then, I was thankful that he didn't probe any further. If I was pressed, I figured I could talk about working on a dairy. We had a few dairy cows and I was familiar with milking them. I was learning to think quick on my feet, to cover myself if I had to lie. Still, I wasn't able to breathe again until he moved on to ask other students questions.

* * *

The scenery just out of Everett is not phenomenal, especially compared to the trip through the North Cascades. There, I looked down a steep gorge and up at a snow-speckled peak. It seemed just feet above there was an alpine meadow. Everyone says this is a terrific train route. It includes a massive tunnel built before the Great Depression. The tunnel is so long that early on, the engineers and conductors were in danger of asphyxiation from the smoke that rolled forth from the big engines. A fan was placed in the tunnel for the safety of all on board. Of course, now, the tunnel has modern venting. We had listened to an announcer explain all this over the intercom as we plunged into the darkness.

13 Law of the Medes and Persians

Stability, also settle, remain firm, weather the storm,
establishment, fixture: 150,
Roget's Thesaurus.

The seventh Nolan commandment, Thou shalt keep steady one's roots.

2009, Katie, near Glasgow, Montana. I reversed my route out of Seattle in order to go the northern route through Glacier again. After the park, there are these spaces of Montana that carry the eye forever. It is as if I could escape everything in this openness, drift outside of time, detached from relationship turmoil.

I've failed at two marriages, and one long-term affair (with Gerald). If I'm going to understand what went wrong, how my family past is connected to my relationship disasters, then I'll need to face each failure squarely. Wasn't it Einstein that said that repeating over and over what's failed the first time is the epitome of foolishness?

* * *

"I thought you were raised poor," Gerald, had said, a slight frown of puzzlement crossing his forehead, causing the front of his black Lenin-style cap to bob ever so slightly.

He makes this comment as I show him the twenty acres my mother still owns, pointing out the large curly maple still standing by the south fence line. We are standing under the maple and looking up at the gently sloping land, still covered with fir, cedar, and the ubiquitous undergrowth of the Pacific Northwest. There is a play of light and shadow on the ground beneath the maple as the leaves quiver in the light breeze.

It is late spring and birds flit above us, tree to tree. "People in my country are rich if they have land. My family was considered wealthy because of our estate."

"Well, my parents had a big mortgage and struggled to pay it."

"Still..." then he changed the subject from land to what he had observed the night before, when we had shown slides of our family travel. "And you travelled a lot. Montana. Wyoming. The slides, they looked like an average white, middle class family to me."

I continually try to explain myself to Gerald.

"We didn't have much," I say a bit uncertainly. I am already struggling against his look of disbelief. "We travelled and camped. Gas was cheap back then and we took our food along."

"Still looked like a middle class vacation to me." He perseveres, and in some ways, I couldn't completely blame him for not understanding. It was a uniquely, and mostly white, American experience, completely out of context for a black man from Nigeria. Road trips and camping with a tent with U.S.A. printed in big letters across one side. In our case a crude army tent, and family lore had it that Dad had stolen it when he left the military. We carried an old rusted Coleman stove. But I am silenced by Gerald's last comment, some lead settled in the pit of my stomach. When I continue I know I sound lame.

"Well, we didn't have money for clothes or school supplies unless we earned it ourselves in summers, berry picking, or by doing odd jobs. If we needed a pencil we had to earn money to buy it." He shrugs dismissively. I notice how out of place he looks, standing in the brush, bits of mud clinging to his black polished shoes, a small bit of briar snagging on his wool suit jacket with his starched white collar peeking out

I twist my hair on top of my head with my fingers. I look at my dishevelled reflection in the train window, then, focus on a young mother wearing faded jeans and a red T-shirt, struggling with a squirming toddler on her lap. She gets out of the seat across the aisle and looks at me apologetically for the squealing child. I smile back reassuringly to let her know I am not bothered in the least. I pick up the child's blankets from the aisle, fold them, and give them back to her when she has a free hand. I hold up the teddy bear retrieved from the aisle and pretend-hide behind it until the child laughs.

"How old is she?" I ask.

"Two-and-a-half," her mother answers. For the next twenty minutes, before she gets off at Wolf Point, we chat like travellers do, finding out that she has grandparents in Billings, and, that they lived near my Aunt Veda.

Eventually, I manage to shake off my uncomfortable memories. Gerald's critical words. His frown.

"Look!" someone on the train calls out. "An elk." We must be somewhere near West Glacier by now. Everyone in the dining car looks the direction they are pointing. We see the towering mountains with their peaks and shiny glaciers flashing in the sun. We catch the fleeting views of the tops of the mountains, then gaze down the deep green gorge with a ribbon of a river at the bottom, and we share a sense of grandeur as if this landscape is part of us.

As we roll slowly over a high trestle, I enjoy eating a leisurely meal of roasted herb chicken, mashed potatoes, and squishy soft white rolls slathered with butter. My friends know me as a vegetarian, but I fall totally off the wagon on this trip. I feel a little sense of shame for eating the flesh of the chicken, noticing what looks like a spot of blood when I cut down to the bone.

I can't eat any more of the meat but savor the mashed potatoes and gravy. I fork the gravy that is dripping down the side of the mound, catching a lump of potato on the way up, then plunging all into the bird's nest at the center. I bend down cautiously to take the bite being careful not to lose any of the extra gravy dripping around the tines of the fork.

Earlier, I had noted the town's names: Whitefish, Havre, Wolf Point. Each town reminds me of trips I took with my family as a child. At little museums we learned things written on painted plywood signs:

The indigenous people near Havre ran bison over a cliff to increase their food supply. Wolf Point Stampede is the oldest rodeo in Montana.

No matter how difficult it was to find the time and the money, my father would say, "We've gotta go visit family back there, pay attention to our roots." Back there was in Idaho, Wyoming, Nebraska, and Montana, family scattered across these states so that upon reaching a destination no matter how small their home, they would always find a way to put us up, sometimes on a porch, and sometimes in a tent in their front yard. Occasionally, it was to go see Aunt Veda in Billings, Montana, with her wide wrap-a-round porch. Or Aunt Maggie in Nebraska, with her hand water pump out in the dusty yard.

I pick up my pen and write down my memories of more family lore, wondering why I simply cannot share any of this with Gerald.

If Gerald would listen, I'd tell him about Uncle Dutch, in his short-legged baggy Wrangler's held up by red suspenders. How Uncle Dutch was commenting on the single tree out there, when we all visited Aunt Maggie to-gether, and how that didn't give much shade. "Boy, were we impressed when Aunt Maggie fired up her old wood stove in that 107 degree heat and fried chicken for all of us," he'd reminded us later. I'd tell Gerald how that huge wood cooking stove overwhelmed the space in Aunt Maggie's kitchen, and how that tiny shack in the middle of nowhere in Nebraska sat like a minute dab of brown in the middle of the yellow prairie. I'd tell him how they went without. I'd know he didn't care to hear about it.

I'd share with Gerald that I'm not sure how Aunt Wandah met Uncle Dutch. But I was told that Dutch's brother, Alcane Woods, met his wife when he was out trapping. He married an indigenous woman and had folks in a band up in Canada. I never got to go visit them, but I heard a story, later, about my parents going up there with Uncle Dutch and Aunt Wandah and being welcomed like long-lost relatives.

I'd tell Gerald how some stories, like Uncle Alcane's, were told over and over: It was a hard winter, and so he sent his wife in from the wilderness, to be taken care of by the band, but didn't go in himself, staying in the cabin and starving to death. That was just the way it was then.

After such a tragic story, Uncle Dutch would lighten things up with his myriad pithy statements: "Did ya hear about that guy whose suspenders were so tight, that when they let loose he shot straight up in the air?" Uncle Dutch always got us laughing till our bellies ached.

I'd tell Gerald how we often went to visit family. Shared stories. How Dad wondered aloud, "Why don't people go visit their folks anymore, like they used to?"

I'd explain to Gerald how we were able to travel to visit Dad's side of the family, with three children in the back seat of a Volkswagen, how we were one of the first to get the people's car, a trailer hooked on with a small hitch and loaded with boxes of home canned food, tent, and camp stove.

I'd explain how camping was on the edge of some farmer's field, one of whom came out to visit our tent with a gun carried casually at his side. My father was quick to explain our trip, saying, "folks don't visit family like they used to," and the farmer ended up being friendly and joining us for breakfast, pancakes cooked in bacon grease on the Coleman stove, and loaded with syrup. I'd tell Gerald how the pancakes were burnt on the edges, crisp with bacon grease, and delicious.

And I'd tell him how before we had the Volkswagen, we travelled like real hicks in the back of the pickup, sitting on an old mattress, Mom constantly waving back at us kids to settle down. Between us kids waving and hollering out the back and the spectre of the homemade plywood camper, we were quite a sight! Then, I'd feel the anxiety of trying to explain myself—why do I have to?

It was, of course, on these visits that I heard the stories of my father being on the road as a hobo. I think I get it now. It is the frustration and the discomfort that comes from my inability to explain to Gerald who I am through telling about my background. Does he even try to know who I am? And I have never been invited to meet his family or friends, so how can I know who he is?

Would his family laugh uproariously at silly jokes like mine does? A bit out of character one day, and after we were all grown, Mom told a joke.

"An elderly couple went to the doctor," she began. "The woman went in first and was answering all of the doctor's questions: Anything unusual?

Have you developed headaches? Have you noticed any unusual growths on your skin? Have you experienced dizziness recently? Do you still have intercourse? The old woman had answered all the questions, except, on that last one she paused. Wait, she said. I'll have to go ask my husband."

"The old lady asked the doctor to wait a minute and she leaned her head out into the waiting room. Dear, do we still have intercourse?"

"No, her husband responded. Don't you remember? We have Blue Cross!"

All of us were taken by surprise by our usually puritanical Mom and began to chuckle, then roar, tears rolling down our cheeks, our chair legs creaking and shaking as we shook with laughter. Mom laughed right along with us, the ties of her yellow plaid apron coming loose as she bent over from the hilarity.

All right. Maybe now I can at least partially answer the question, What's at stake? Gerald cannot relate to my odd background. He can't understand how it feels to come from a hillbilly background, complete with memories of shotgun weddings and stills next door, then find yourself in a job in academia, struggling to relate to your peers. It's about class differences. When I told my writing mentor, Mickey, she still wasn't satisfied. "I just don't buy that," Mickey said. "There is something urgent you are leaving out. Perhaps a childhood trauma?"

I was fuming. It *is* about class differences. How could she make such a judgement? We all have childhood traumas! Some memories are best left alone.

If Mickey weren't always stylishly dressed, with the latest boots, and a hat perfect for her outfit, and, if she didn't have such a feminine voice, with a lovely response tic, "Okay, sweetie," I know I'd shout at her. As it is, my fuming diffuses, and I am totally charmed. Does she realize that she is risking an outburst from me?

14 Gaudy as a Peacock

Ostentation, also: clean the outside of the platter, tomfoolery: 882, Roget's Thesaurus, 1947.

The eighth Nolan commandment, Thou shalt not put on airs.

2009, Katie, Chicago, Illinois to McCook, Nebraska. I am getting close to Chicago, after rolling through North Dakota and Minnesota, and I can almost hear my father saying, "Them bulls was tough. Times was hard." He had also told me a story of how him and Uncle Charlie had met up once in Chicago. It was there that they had been playing cards in a pool hall, then some guy rose from his chair saying: "Hey, you is cheatin'." That was when my father and Uncle Charlie "went backin' outta there, with Uncle Charlie holdin' a knife." Then, he looked at Uncle Charlie and said, "You was cheatin?" Charlie grinned. He had decided to head out on the rails without Uncle Charlie after that.

He always told his scrapes with such understatement. It turns out that they had been playing cards with the mafia and they were lucky to get out of there alive.

Chicago train station with all its cool, hard surfaces. The hub of America where all train lines lead out like spokes going south, west, and west again, just a little further south, and yet west again, a bit further south yet. There is an exuberance to it that brings to mind the way I felt as a child, rolling down the pasture hill, eyes wide open to watch for cow pies and ant hills, over and over until I was flat on my back at the bottom with the world twirling above, clouds and sky and horizon rushing in a circle. I knew it was the hub my father had often travelled through, hard-scrabbling and hungry.

It is a six hour stopover in Chicago, the whole time of which I plan to spend at the station. The Chicago station has a wonderful contrast between its turn-of-the-century ceiling of pressed tin, old marble floors, and the wooden pew seats, then, the rows of modern little shops and restaurants down one hallway. I whiled away several hours at a coffee shop, reading last month's Chicago Tribune and watching people. The headline, blocked neatly over the date, July 21, 2009, states "Bailout exposure: $24 trillion." The article is focused on the government's program to bail out banks and big business, and I wonder how each person is faring as I listen to the sound of the crowds echoing from all the hard surfaces.

While I am lost in thought a youngish man (maybe 55, odd what seems young when you pass age 60) approaches my table. I feel nervous and glance away but he catches my eye anyway. Usually, it is easy for me to just politely dismiss a stranger, but for some reason I don't this time. Perhaps it is those hazel eyes, more green than not, with his hunter green shirt open just so at the neck. Hazel eyes and dark hair, trim at the hips, along with that Irish look. That always attracts me. They say we are drawn to the familiar and that seems to be true in my case, because this is the look of many of the men in my extended family.

"So, what do you think of the headlines?" He smiles and I notice the thin line of his mouth.

"I was just wondering how all these people are doing? Are they going to survive?" I answer, then go on, as he seems to be waiting. "It is so similar to the Depression. In the 1930's when the railroad barons began to use their monopoly to hike up prices to transport the crops, farmers were quick to use their organizations of co-op and grange to appeal to the government for railroad regulation and relief in the battle. So why are they seemingly so anti-regulation and pro-big business now?" I pause, regretting that I sound a bit like I am lecturing a class.

"We have to give tax breaks and subsidies to big business to keep them in our states and to create more jobs, right?" He peers at me, frowning a little, but I go on, as he tentatively sits down.

"Reminds me of a husband threatening his wife that, if she doesn't allow him to pimp her out, he'll just go to another woman. He threatens to leave her for someone more willing. Maybe states, even nations, should band together, be uniform or even refuse tax breaks and corporate benefits, and seek liberation from this corporate blackmail. Why don't they? Down with the corporate pimps!" I'm sitting on the edge of my chair by this time and I want to shout at him. No! I just want to get him to stop staring at me. Then, I feel embarrassed at the emotion. I push myself back in the chair and sit up straight.

Keeping my spine aligned, feet spaced evenly on the floor, the way I'd been taught in a zen lesson, I continue: "There is the basic argument that government should invest in business. In fact Calvin Coolidge informed the populace that 'The business of government is business.' The familiar logic is that if business is gaining lots of capital, with government bailouts if necessary, it will create jobs." I'm reminding myself to breathe evenly.

"Right. Old Calvin Coolidge had it figured out. Government bailouts. Trickle down economy. Should work now." He is still causing me to come a bit unstitched with that grin. But I am not going to go all girl on him, and defer to his logic.

"But why don't we use a bottom logic? If government invests in workers and the middle class, people will buy goods, and when they buy goods, business will get going, producing more goods. So bail the people out! The fact is, businesses won't invest in expansion, hiring workers in the process, unless someone is buying what they are producing. In fact, this logic was applied by Franklin Delano Roosevelt, and it seemed to work better than Coolidge's theory. So why, as we head into the greatest recession since the Great Depression, do we stick with Coolidge's ideology? It is all a mystery to me." I gaze at him, wait for a response.

"Well, you're sure opinionated!" He shakes his head and rises to leave. I want to say, wait, we can disagree. But I sit stunned. Why did I do that? Here I am, breaking the Nolan commandment that I should not be a show-off by being so arrogant with my opinions. "What a bunch of tomfoolery," my parents would say. My mother, especially, would say, "Don't be a smarty pants. You're acting too big for your britches!"

That certainly is not how to make a friend of a man who has a cute grin and is flirting with you. And where is that tolerance I always hope for in others? All I can do is sigh. Acknowledge that I simply do not know how to flirt. Chastened, I bury myself in the world news section of the paper.

Exhausted from the long layover, I miss most of Iowa, catching up on sleep. It is a relief to be back on the train. After we enter Nebraska I am wide awake and notice the familiar towns—Lincoln, Hastings, Holdredge. I'd like to talk to someone about all the things that keep swimming in my head after the long stopover, but I'm afraid to engage anyone. The conversation with that cute man still stings.

One good thing on the layover. I got an email from Steve Anderson. Nice guy in my writing class. And I wonder why he is actually writing to me!

Dear Katie,

Thank you for sharing your personal stories in writing class. I just felt the disappointment of that young woman, as she struggled through her experiences with the men in her life. And when I read how dismal her treatment was when she had sex with Gerald, I almost cried. That was so sad. When I return I would like to meet. Your comments on my writing were so helpful. Could we do that?
Yours,
Steve

Dear Steve,

I am grateful for your sensitive comments about my writing. Sometimes I become confused, and I'm not sure if I'm really capturing what went on. Most likely I am not being fair to Gerald. You know what I mean, how it takes two to tango, all that. I have a new insight-- our differences do make the relationship difficult, but that is neither his fault nor mine. In any case, thanks.
Yours,
Katie

Dear Katie,

I am in Shimonoseki, Japan. The last day of class you asked me to email you about my experiences with zen masters, saying that you had spent some time in Japan yourself. I think I may sound ridiculous when I describe what's happening here, so you can skim through this, glaze over now and stop reading, or just read the first sentence of each paragraph. I will never know.

I think my first attempts at finding a teacher are some of the most revealing instances of how silly I am. After my first week here, I spent my three days off going from temple to temple, asking in the worst Japanese possible, "Where can I find a zen teacher?" At each temple I was warmly and formally welcomed with much bowing. I was sat down at a kotatsu (low table) and given tea and sweets and asked about myself. Good, I thought, an interview before taking on a student, thinking proudly that I was like Jack Kornfield or somebody. Soon to be made ripe with wisdom that I could share in my next book. Au contraire.

I was soon sent on my way with no further invitation, no introduction to a zen master (or was that host the master?), and no encouragement to come back.

I began to think I had not shown enough humility, recalling a documentary I had seen where the young initiates sat on the temple doorstep through rough weather for days, until they were taken in. So the next temple

I found, I researched it beforehand and discovered they held a sitting practice based on Soto-Shu zen (just sitting) at 5:30 daily. I got up at 4:30 the next day, made my way up the mountain on ancient stone steps, noting the bamboo groves I passed, swaying in the wind. And hearing the thump, thump, thump in a steady rhythm, of a drum.

When I arrived at the temple, I could not summon the courage to go in, opting to sit on the porch instead. Then, fearing I'd be seen and shooed away, I slipped into the adjoining graveyard. By now, my heart is clanging with fear. But each morning I went, hearing the drum on my way up the mountain, fearing I would be discovered and run off the mountain, and, well, just plain fear next to the graves.

Then one morning I mustered the courage to slide open the shoji screens and was greeted calmly by the master.

He handed me a zafu, showed me how to carry it clutched to my chest and led me to the meditation hall. We descended into silence. At least he did. My mind was a racer, you know, off and running like it had been given the flag at the Indianapolis 500. I returned for three weeks before I got up the courage to ask my burning question: Is it possible to know the meaning of life?" His response: "Do you have to know right now?" My response: "Yes."
His response: "Yes."
Make of it what you will.
Puzzled,
Steve

I was considerably cheered by Steve's emails. Another way to keep my mind busy and away from difficult topics?

In any case, being busy with my "bottom up, not trickle down" ranting leaves me with very little memory of my relationships, of what went wrong, of who they were and who I was at the time. Instead of a full memory, my recall is like a hummingbird's, darting in and out, zipping away after barely tasting the experience. I even feel guilty spending a lot of time on it, on my own little world, when there are these really BIG problems out there.

I do allow myself to think about my little world in my personal journal. I look at a portion written in 1995 during my two years at SUNY, Binghamton, working on my doctorate in philosophy:

State University New York, Binghamton. I followed my dream, returned to school at forty-five years old. When I told a friend of my hesitation, that I would be fifty when I finished graduate school, she said, well in five years you'll be fifty in any case. For some reason that convinced me to go. I want to get a doctorate in philosophy and learn to write, I'd told her. Crazy idea when I think about it now. Maybe crazier than Kerouac's Neal Cassady, spinning naked like a top in the middle of a street.

I add a note, some letters a bit scraggly, as the tracks aren't very smooth at the moment:

And don't you also see, Mickey? Men aren't very comfortable when the woman has a higher degree than them. It is about my having a PhD.

I can't believe she doesn't accept any of my reasoning about why I'm not living my love story! In spite of what Mickey says, I still insist, I am having difficulty with Gerald because of class differences. And I have had difficulty with other men because of my PhD. I argued this repeatedly with Mickey before I left on my trip (leaving out my usual anti-trickle down rant), and she always responded, "I just don't buy it."

"Okay, then, it has to do with men not accepting that I am a woman with lots of opinions," I always argued. "There's something more," Mickey often repeated. "That's not quite it either," she often added. Then, I wanted to shout back, "What, then?" But I would just sigh and nod.

I managed to keep my frustration under wraps. I avoided speaking with Mickey until I thought I could sound gracious.

Looking up and seeing the station sign, "McCook, Nebraska," I remember this little story my father told me about going to Mom's fiftieth class reunion in Hillsboro, Oregon.

Everyone around the table related where they'd gone to college and Dad said he'd mumbled "Nebraska," not knowing what else to say. I realized then that Dad would have liked to go to college. Yet, he did get an education on the road. Perhaps the hobo philosophy he shared is why I was drawn to studying philosophy. I'll get to that and leave the question that tortures me, What's at stake? for later.

15 Stand on a Volcano

Danger, also dangerous course, leap in the dark,
sit on a barrel of gunpowder: 665,
Roget's Thesaurus, 1947.

It could probably be shown by facts and figures that there is no distinctly native criminal class except Congress.

—Mark Twain

1932, Bud, Tampa, Florida. I had made it all the way up to Charlottesville, hitched my way to Richmond, Virginia (or "Virginny" was the way locals said it), then dropped down to Tampa. It was back in Georgia, or maybe Alabama, a couple years back, that I first met up with Harry, when we both got took up onto that chain gang.

At first sight I'd taken a liking to him. Maybe it was the broad, ready smile and bright blue eyes. Then, there was the fact that Harry was tall, blonde, and lean, "a big Swede" was how someone described him, and he was my opposite; people said I was stocky and barrel-chested like a dark Irishman. Or maybe it was because Harry was pretty much cheerful all the time. Harry was about ten years older than me and had been on the road off and on about that much longer. But he was different from some of the other hobos. He had a political purpose.

Harry was an organizer for the Wobblies. He would often begin his sentences with,"You know, Bud, that no man should have someone in authority over him?"

"Yeah, that's for sure," I would usually respond. Or, sometimes I would say: "That's about right, Harry."

"So, that is what the Wobblies believe." Usually, that would be the end of the conversation but one time I decided to say a little more and Harry, startled, turned his head and stared, mouth wide open.

"Seems like any group of guys come together, there's some guy there who tries to get it over the others, lord it over them."

"Exactly," Harry enthused. He decided to try a different tack. "But they won't be able to hold that position for long if they don't have the government, the police, or a military to back them up, the way the Carnegies and the Rockefellers do." Harry is really getting wound up now.

"I s'pose," I shrugged.

Harry, now a little frustrated with another of my short answers comes back with, "Jeez, Bud! You seem angry enough to stop some guy in his tracks and cause him to shit his pants—but all's I see you do is smile. Don't you ever yell at anyone?"

"Humph. Nope, ain't inclined to waste my breath yelling." This is all that Harry's gonna get. But I respected Harry and began thinking about the things he'd told me about the IWW. Rumor had it that lots of 'em were foreigners and lots of 'em were anarchists. Not Harry though. American through and through, and he tended toward more traditional socialism, he'd said. If one could dub him as an anarchist, it would be an anarcho-syndicalist he'd added. That is, through unions the workers could down capitalism and finally be free of exploitation. It was the first time I'd learned all this and I had Harry to thank for that.

We'd stayed in the jungle together for several days, resting up and telling stories. It was that night we decided to deck a freight out. We weren't that far out of Tampa before we came to another, smaller yard.

The dusk left the maze of rails in the freight yard looking dark and ominous. There were low clouds and the smell of soon-coming rain mixed with the diesel smell of the yard. Two men, armed with clubs and holstered guns, walked out of the shack, talking boisterously:

"This freight's got all the field hands on it. They ought'a be loaded. They likely just got paid."

"All we gotta do is quick slide the door shut, then bring 'em out at gun point."

These were the railroad bulls that had made it a habit of robbing us 'bos, just after we all got paid for the latest harvest. It had become a common practice, as more and more bulls were recruited from jail cells by the railroad barons. The bulls made up the barons' own private army, was the way Harry put it, a legal mercenary group, compliments of U.S. Congress.

Me and Harry saw the two men as our boxcar rolled into the yard. We shouted to the other men. "Bulls!" It was too late. The car stopped and the door rolled shut. "We know you're all in there. Come out one by one with your hands up! We won't mind shooting any one of ya." We all filed out, forming a half circle below the door of the boxcar. "Don't move! If we see a muscle move, we'll drop ya."

"You. Don't move." A bullet whizzed by me and I heard the bull repeat, "I said, don't move."

Rage rose up when I saw the older 'bo next to me drop. They didn't have to kill him! He was old, and he couldn't hold still. He just fidgeted. But I couldn't let them see my anger. I stood as still as a statue and my face went blank.

"Now, hand over your stash, all of you, or more of you's gonna die." The men reached into their pockets and handed over all the pay from their last job. I pulled my pay from my pocket, mentally cursing myself for not having sewn it into my hatband.

"Get back in that boxcar and we don't wanna see ya again." We climbed back in, some rushing from fear, and the door pushed shut with a hard shove from one of the bulls. We heard the metal bar click across the door.

"What are we gonna do?" This from Harry in a half-whisper. "Wait 'til they're gone." I murmured. "Don't have much choice."

We all sat still in the silence, eight men, only hearing the noise of connections being made between the cars. New boxcars were being added to the train. Finally, after what seemed like twenty minutes, a young 'bo stood up, impatient. "We gotta get out of this car."

"How's that gonna happen?" Another 'bo responded, a bit sarcastically.

"Look, there's likely to be other 'bos hiding out below the cars, or maybe even in the next boxcar. We should all just shout. They'll hear and let us out. We gotta get out. I heard of 'em setting these boxcars on a side rail and letting the men inside die of the heat and lack of water."

"Yeah. Well, raising a ruckus is likely to get us killed. We don't know if it'll be 'bos or bulls that come running." Now all the men were responding, some a little louder, some still in half-whispers.

"Look," said Harry, as he looked steadily at me to get my agreement, "We can either ride on out of here, in which case, we'll all be broke and hungry, or we can take a chance and pile outta this boxcar, and go after 'em and get our money back."

"Are you crazy?" The men were murmuring and some shrunk back against the walls of the boxcar.

"Well, that's our choices. We don't got many. It's 80 degrees out there and it ain't likely to cool down tonight. Even getting outta here, we can go hungry for days, 'til we get to the next job—and some of us might die of the heat if these doors are shut tight. Or, we can risk it, get the money, and have food 'til we get to our next job."

"I'm in," I said. No one else responded. By then a 'bo in the yard had heard the ruckus and slid the door open. All the men scattered toward the bushes 'cept me and Harry. The two of us didn't say another word. We were downright driven. It was not that we didn't care about staying alive, just that we couldn't let this stand. Not much choice. Hunger, or risk our lives. Both of us were tired of being hungry. Sometimes I had pretended that the empty gnawing warn't there. But worse than the hole in the gut is the feeling of legs like lead, so heavy that a man has to force himself to count the steps he takes to keep 'em moving. Then the gut wrenches and the legs twitch from the effort, and a guy just keeps counting and grimacing forward. I decided to fight.

"Here, take these." One of the 'bos steps from the bushes and holds a gun in one hand and a club in another.

"Don't want no gun," I said. "That'll get ya in a heap more trouble than a club."

99

"How's about another club?" The man disappeared for a moment and came back with a club.

I glanced over at Harry as we slipped up on the railroad shack, the place where the bulls hung out. Harry nodded. We crouched by the window, unmoving, lest the sound of gravel under our boots gave us away, and listened to the bulls talking.

"Did you see the way that guy dropped. Good aim, Joe, 'cause he died on the spot." The bulls were drinking and the big one, weighing in at around two hundred pounds, and resting his shotgun against his knees, was the one complimenting Joe. We were just feet from the bulls so their voices boomed.

"He ain't the first one," Joe said, with a self-satisfied smile. "Why, I've killed at least a dozen bums," he bragged. "How 'bout you, Jim?"

Jim chimed in, "I've got my share, all you gotta do is place a bouncing piece of metal on the tracks and watch 'em scream and get knocked off and ground up under the train."

"A little 'bo hamburger," Joe laughed.

Pretty soon the drink got them laughing harder and harder at what they'd done to 'bos and then their talk turned to women. "There ain't many women decking a train. Wouldn't I like to see that," Joe said. "I wouldn't make her into hamburger, for awhile anyways, until I tasted the meat."

"Aw, Joe, that's the only way you're gonna get some."

I readied myself to carry out the plan me and Harry had made.

The shack for the bulls was warm with plenty of wood stacked up, and the heat and drinking put all four of them into a stupor. The big one had rolled out on his coat in the corner, passed out. Joe and Jim were still sitting by the fire with their backs to the door. Another bull, who hadn't said much, was lazy drunk, but still awake.

When silence fell and me and Harry could hear snoring, we nodded. We slipped around the corner, still crouching, then stood, and looked through the small window at the top of the door. Each of us was carrying a club, and knew we could take the two dozing by the fire, hoping we didn't wake the guy on the floor, or rouse the one half-asleep, slumped against the catty-cornered wall.

At another nod, we burst through the door, clubbed the two by the stove over the head. It came quick and hard and it sounded like the same sickening thud I had heard when I'd hit the guard on the chain gang. The bulls toppled off their chairs without a sound. By this time, the big guy in the corner was sitting up and had drawn a bead on us, shouting, "Hey, down on the floor." We went down.

We were pinned to the floor with a gun on us. The quiet bull was awake. He pulled his gun on the big bull and shouted, "Drop it!"

Me and Harry rose slowly, me saying, "Hey, thanks," still puzzling out what had happened. Harry asked, "Are you a bull? I mean, I never seen no bull siding with 'bos."

"Well, not for long. I was caught stealing a cow. My family was hungry, and I was offered this job if I wanted outta prison. I didn't know what to do but I wanted to feed my family. Now, I reckon, I won't be feeding them. I just couldn't stomach no more killing."

An odd silence came over all of us. Maybe we was all thinking about the trap we was in.

"Look," I broke the silence, "It ain't gonna happen that way. You're going with us, let things cool off down here, then we'll find a place where you can send for your wife and kids."

"Yeah," Harry chimed in, "you're coming with us. We'll just wait to see which way the land lies, then figure out what we're gonna do." Beforehand, me and Harry had agreed that neither of us would kill anyone, so we knocked the big guy out, and skedaddled, back to the jungle, back to the guys who'd just lost everything they'd had to eat on till the next job. Some had been run off by the bulls, so we couldn't give all the loot back.

We gave the extra share to the family man. I felt like a decent guy again, part of the human race. Sure, I hadn't always done the right thing. But never again, I vowed.

Then, we caught the next freight out. To avoid trouble, me and Harry and the former bull knew to avoid Tampa for a good spell of time.

16 Brought Up at the Feet of Gamaliel

Scholar, also learned man, intelligentsia, Dr. Pangloss: 492,
Roget's Thesaurus, 1947.

1932, Bud, riding out of Tampa. Me and Harry decked the next train going north. We rode alone for two hours and began to relax, once we'd passed through Georgia and gotten our distance between us and the cynical bulls.

"Got while the gettin' was good," chuckles Harry. "Yep, like to have heard what they said when we left."

"Probably not much. They wouldn't want to admit a couple of 'bos like us got 'em. They'd never tell how they got the worst of it." I went silent and Harry always respected a guy's need for privacy. That's one of the things I liked about Harry. He wasn't about to probe. He respects a man enough to listen and take it in, but not to demand more.

"You know, Harry, sometimes a man doesn't do what he thinks he should. Then, he'll regret it all his life. Always wished he'd done something different. But it's too late."

"Yeah, well we all carry some regret. We're bound to when we're pushed about, this way and that. You ain't always free to do what you think you should. You get pushed into things, then regret them afterwards. Can't let things get to ya. Ya know, they'd like all of us dead, just as soon as they'd look

102

at us. No need of us helping 'em make us miserable by going around regretting what we should've done. Probably couldn't have done anything different, anyhow, and lived to tell about it."

"Well a guy can get to feeling he can't trust himself. Then, once you don't trust yourself, you pretty much don't trust no one." I stopped speaking suddenly but hoped Harry would fill the silence. Sometimes silence shakes ya more than the words of a man.

"You were something back there," Harry said, trying to change the tone, make us both feel a bit more cheery.

It worked. I don't know what I'd do without Harry! A guy alone on the road could go crazy. No one to look out for him, nobody to talk to. We both was silent now. It was understood between us that we should quit talking. Too much feeling, ain't no good on the road.

I looked down at the plywood floor. It was vibrating as we hit a rough patch in the tracks. I wanted to find a place to be alone, but that warn't always easy on the road.

Me and Harry decided to beat our way west. We cut through Cincinnati, then Chicago, and on to Denver. We made a short stop in Denver, then hitched our way back up into Wyoming.

We was riding in the back of a rancher's truck. We'd been quiet for awhile and Harry dozed off on his bindle, his head bouncing near the back of the cab. In the silence, I noticed the land. Miles of scrub formed the horizon outside the truck bed, a cattle range in Wyoming. Endless sky shifted from a darker blue to a pastel as it neared the horizon. Lean-to wooden snow fences dotted the nearby landscape along the rutted road. Far in the distance, rolling hills seemed to sing bass, like I'd heard the deep bass of a guy in a barbershop quartet. It was like those mountains flung themselves up high, and if they could sing they'd be changing to tenor by early winter, when snow dotted the top of the peaks. I was looking out on the land, dreaming a little of owning some property one day, right up against some mountains like those. I could rest, a fortress behind me. I'd be free. Then, a thought that sunk my stomach: *I am a fugitive. I can never settle down.*

It was gonna be a long, cold winter in a Wyoming bunkhouse. The floor of rough boards could install a sliver in your foot, so I careful-like walked across it in my socks full of holes, first thing each morning, to go fetch my boots by the stove, put there to keep 'em from freezing. Even then, they were stiff and cold and I had to struggle to push 'em on, made even harder 'cause of m' flat feet. The bunkhouse had three bunks lining each side and this left a narrow corridor in the center, so us men had to carefully avoid each other as we stirred about to get ready for work.

The rancher hired six men to move his cattle to lower ground. But he had refused to hire both Harry and me, saying that two guys travelling together could mean trouble.

"I ain't taking the job without ya so let's just move on." I wasn't gonna let on, but it felt like Harry was gonna abandon me, the way those hobos did my first camp.

"No, no, that ain't practical. Best take that job and when ya catch up to me again you will have something for both of us to eat on." I knew Harry was not expecting me to share what I earned with him and had just said that to get me to stay on. And I 'sposed he was right. I could catch up with him after a spell. It still felt bad, though, separating again.

So Harry'd had to hitch a ride back into Colorado, where he was gonna catch a freight out of Denver.

As he left, Harry'd said that maybe we could catch up with each other again down south. Said he had some work to do down in Florida, where things were tough for workers. This knowledge was goin' to create a dangerous situation, sometime in the near future, but for the time being, we'd gone our separate ways.

17 Dull as a Beetle

Dejection, also prostration of soul, grin a ghastly
smile, dull as ditchwater: 837,
Roget's Thesaurus, 1947.

The ninth Nolan commandment, Thou shalt get on with it.

2009, Katie, Los Angeles. The guy wearing camouflage pants and sitting on the seat directly across the aisle retreats into his gun magazine. He is hunching his shoulders, wrapping his arms around his belly in a protective position. I wonder if he's an Iraqi vet. I take in his eyes which are unfocussed and jumpy, the way a cornered critter looks. Uncomfortable, I shift my attention onto my writing.

Mickey says that we ought to consider our character's worst fear. I used to think that my father's worst fear was loss of freedom. Don't join anything. Stay free and independent.

However, I'm not certain anymore that literal loss of freedom was his worst fear. I'm not completely sure what it was, but I think he may have hit upon it when he was talking about being beaten down so your spirit is crushed. It is loss of existential freedom. That is, we might be free, in a sense, to choose ourselves, as John Paul Sartre puts it. But sometimes something is done to us that causes a loss of this freedom, a freedom at our very core, the freedom to be who we will be. It is the loss of freedom through oppression.

I am startled when I think of this. Of course! This is the freedom my father feared losing. He just would never quote Sartre to explain himself. Or rather the later Sartre, after Sartre corrected himself due to the input of Simone DeBeauvoir (leave it to a woman to get an understanding of oppression right), explaining to him that existential freedom finds its limit when oppression, particularly women's oppression, but men's too, rears its ugly head, oftentimes sending men and women into a lifetime of poverty.

The train lumbers along near Sacramento, where I have arrived from McCook, after switching back west on the route through Iowa, Nebraska, Colorado, Utah, and Nevada. So here I am back on the west coast, passing through California (Californy rings in my head from my father's voice and the way he always played with words), and I will soon be enjoying once again the scenery on the Coast Starlight. The train slows to let a freight whizz by, so I get that sense of vertigo again. Once the freight passes, I suddenly see palm trees. It is Santa Barbara, a paradise on earth!

White sand. Warmth. My father would have loved this place, and I remember him describing how he spent his days off from picking fruit, bobbing about in the waves of the Pacific Ocean. Thinking about that image leaves a little tug at my heart, feeling Dad's struggle and his determination.

Dad's modelling of strength and humor in the face of all of that oppression is why I feel embarrassed to this day to admit that at one time I'd taken such an emotional tumble that I wasn't certain whether I would ever get up again. And it was over something rather trivial, compared to Dad's ill fortune.

I was struggling to make it on my adjunct teacher's salary. My car had broken down, and to add to the sense of Camus-inspired absurdity, the passenger door, which was sprung loose and tied shut with a rope, slipped open as I rounded a curve, right before the engine bit the dust. After that, I sprained my ankle in a fall. I took the bus to work, winced as I crawled up its high steps, maneuvering each step precariously with crutches. Everything was coming unravelled, and I felt as if I were Sisyphus being pushed back by several boulders. Then, there was Gerald.

"We need to take a break," Gerald says. "And I've decided that oral sex is something that I really want." Gerald states this firmly, sitting stiffly forward on the steps of my front porch. He's breaking up with me. Good god. He is breaking up with me because I don't do enough oral sex? I had tried to explain to him that I needed to be really turned on before…

I look down, making sure not to make eye contact, then say, emotionless, "Don't worry, I've already cried about it." I am lying about this because I feel I ought to cry. But I can't. I won't. He looks relieved. Yet, we both know that we will see each other the next day at work. That we will still converse, politely, as if nothing has happened.

Gerald leaves. I am lying flat on the floor of my living room unable to move. I feel as if a bulldozer is sitting on my chest. My mind is blank, except for the thought, *he broke up with me.*

I stare at the darkening windows. I will myself up, hearing my father's voice: "When the going gets tough, the tough get going. Just get on with it." He would not approve. I get up. I force an ironic smile. I limp into the kitchen, and, with one hand on the counter for support, pour myself a glass of milk, grab two oatmeal raisin cookies, gulp it all down.

I call a new friend from Mickey's writing class, Jen Fletcher. "Guess what. Gerald broke up with me again. This time he said that there is not enough oral sex. What kind of a reason is that? If someone loves you they adapt, work things out with you, right? Who would break up with someone because they don't get oral sex?" I am spooning large amounts of Jamoca Almond Fudge ice cream directly from a quart carton into my mouth.

There is a long pause. "Well, that makes sense to me. Don't people deserve to have what they want in bed?"

I can't believe Jen said that. I want to get angry, shout, but don't. Instead, I say, "Really, is that what people think? Maybe I'm just out of touch."

I don't believe a word I say. Always the appeaser.

Jen and I had been introduced by one of the other writing group members. A volunteer for Witness for Peace in Columbia, Jen had joined the writing group but then missed half of the sessions.

Naturally gray, Jen's strong eyebrows bring attention to her dark brown eyes. I admire her narrow shoulders, something I do not have. I've always looked a bit less than petite with the broad shoulders of a German peasant girl, likely inherited from my mother.

We'd enjoyed a few late night outings, drinking Mexican beer graced with lime, and eating burritos at the Chupacabra on Phinney Ridge, one of Jen's favorite places. She is the kind of person that really draws you out. Within weeks, she had ferreted out practically my whole life story. My sorry first marriage. Meeting my first husband while on skates, serving burgers, fries and milkshakes as an A & W carhop. Leaving my second husband to his nightly bar visits to go to Japan and, while there, having an affair with a zen monk. He was oh, so sexy, in that robe and we had gone to a jazz festival on the Japan sea, me and three zen monks. The monks had brought a large cooler with whiskey and ice.

"You had an affair with a zen monk? Probably a little pent up energy there." And Jen starts laughing. By this time, Jen has come over and we both spoon ice cream from cartons.

"Yeah. It all started with losing my shoes."

"Oh, this is going to be good." Jen says.

"I danced with one of them, me twirling and twirling like his robe, him laughing uproariously, the way a happy Buddha is expected to laugh. Some time out there dancing, I shed my shoes never to see them again. Take me home with you, I whispered in his ear. Okay, was all he said."

"A man of few words. I'd like that."

"He didn't know much English—in fact I met him first as his English teacher. He was passionate and said, all night long, come here, come here, his lovely robe hanging on the temple wall."

"You made love in a temple? Wow."

"Yeah, isn't love supposed to be sacred?"

"During one break from sex," I continued, "I asked him for the bathroom and in the dim light I slid open the wrong shoji screen, stepped out one step, and fell out the back of the temple! No problem. He heard my surprised whoa! and gave me a hand back up. There I was, on my knees on the tatami mat as if I was bowing to his Buddha nature."

"So where did it go from there?" Jen is the kind of person who always asks the right questions to encourage someone to talk.

"Well, the head priest of the temple married him off. Evidently, they couldn't visualize an ongoing relationship with the gaijin working out. I actually felt bad about it. Not about the affair but about his getting married and losing our friendship. He didn't return my calls, even though I left him what I thought was a rather zen message: "Please don't worry about it. Just leap over it and see it as another obstacle that is part of the path.""

"That's hilarious. A zen monk. So, why on earth are you staying with this guy Gerald?"

"Well, he's an amazing person, really. He told me once that for whatever reason he feels responsible for the welfare of others. He really cares. He actually risked his life in his country's independence struggle. Only to come to the U.S. later and find himself involved in the civil rights movement here. It's rare to find someone who is that committed."

"You should keep in mind that sometimes a person so in love with *the people* can't really find their way clear to love *a person*." Jen responds.

I sigh a heavy sigh. "Maybe you're right." Still, I couldn't help but think of Gerald's bigger than life past. Something that earned him a scar from a knife in his back. I truly admire him.

"It sounds like you really threw yourself into your zen lessons, and I'm not just talking about the affair with the monk. I've always wanted to practice zen meditation but haven't gotten around to it."

"Well, it's embarrassing, but I think I got distracted by the affair with the monk, um, and another fling with a fellow from England, can't recall his name, so I didn't really learn that much zen." Jen laughs at this confession.

Thinking about being flat on the floor, unable to move, I am reminded of what I learned once from a zen master during that happier moment in my life. "Wake up! Wake up your life!" he'd shouted. Well, easier said than done.

Here I am, only the tiniest ray of light coming in, barely making it off the floor, staggering like a downed boxer. It has got me to wondering whether I really can rid myself of this murky confusion. I want to be fully alive, wake up, be less numb, I really do. I did meditate for a time. Then, due to the constraints of a very busy teaching career, and other distractions, I'd given it up.

Looking back over this chapter I had an aha moment. I am having no luck with relationships because I don't do well with oral sex. The very thing men want most! I couldn't wait to share this insight with Mickey. When I did at our next class, she said, after a long pause and a squinty frown, and in the wake of a few raised eyebrows from the other students, "I really don't think that's it."

* * *

Frustrated from not figuring out what's at stake, I look down at my empty wine glass. Then, I glance out the window of the lounge car. Rows and rows of energy-producing wind machines line up like ghostly skeletons on the bare brown hills. I had been so hopeful when I had been told that wind as an alternative energy source would save us from planetary destruction, then to find out that it is difficult for wind to produce enough energy for our big urban centers. Still, perhaps wind machines can produce enough, given more sophisticated technology. Ah, well. I sigh.

Time has flown and I am stiff and lethargic from sitting in my seat too long. Maybe Mickey will be convinced that oral sex really is my problem if I tell her more about what happened.

18 The Iron Entering into the Soul

Capability of giving pain; also, wound to the quick, stick in one's throat,
harrowing, freeze the blood, chill the spine: 830,
Roget's Thesaurus, 1947.

2009, Katie, Los Angeles. When I leave the L.A. train station, and step out
onto the street, the air is hot and smelly. I gasp. Gray pavement covers the
ground so that there are only patches of earth where the pavement is cut away
to attempt to grow a tree. The deciduous trees appear to be choking.
I sit down at a cafe near the train station and commence writing.

* * *

We had gone to a little hideaway beach cabin several hours from
Seattle. We had started out at 10 PM, me driving, so, unlike Gerald, I was
exhausted when we arrived.

Even so, I do not want to go to bed. There is a sense of sameness and
dread that I try to overcome.

I always know the moment of his orgasm, the tension of his body, the
draining of his tension when he finally releases his sperm into my vagina. The
feeling of his weight when he drifts down. The pleasantness of bodies touching head to toe.

But I do not know his thoughts during seduction. Is he distracted by
some flaw in me?

111

Thinking, I wish she looked more like Beyonce'?

What I don't know is frightening. If fear overtakes me, I have disconnected hormonal sex.

I don't know when trust occurs. Even when the elements of trust begin, doubt creeps in. I become a sex agnostic. A relationship agnostic. The emotions and bonding that occur from sex slip away. Well, really, I become a sex *atheist.*

I tell Gerald that I was raped with a date-rape drug. A man slipped it into my drink when I was in Las Vegas. Another man suddenly appeared, then, with support from them under each armpit, I recall being propelled out of the casino. After that, I have no real memory, no imagery, but somehow I know that men pressed their penises into my drugged, slack mouth. I woke up the next morning on a park bench. Panicked, I ran toward city center. Gerald doesn't comment or hold me, even though we lay side by side in a double bed, both covered to our shoulders with a down comforter.

I find the dark wood panelling of the Copalis Beach hideaway depressing. Gerald has gone into the shower, not singing, not humming, silent. His silence disturbs me.

"How was your shower?" I prop myself up on an elbow as he enters the room in his white terrycloth robe.

"Not bad. Water smells funny."

"I think there is lots of iron in the water on this part of the beach. Or maybe sulfur."

"Maybe so."

Earlier he'd talked and talked about himself. His interactions with students and other professors at Seattle University, what disturbed him, his political outrages. Now, why is he so silent?

He lies completely still beside me. I hear the low hum of the ocean. Notice how dark it is in the room. He makes a move for me, sliding his hand down my thigh and splaying his fingers on my most sensitive part, moving the folds around, making me moist.

Arousal comes in the form of an electrical current buzzing from my waist down, then I drift away from the arousal, slipping into the dark room's energy and emotionally distancing myself from Gerald.

112

He removes his hand and awkwardly drapes it onto my head, pressing it towards his penis.

When I don't respond in the way he desires, he takes an even more awkward position, still presses my head towards his penis, then, with one hand grabs between my legs. I go stiff with terror. I feel nothing, not even the usual sensitivity of masturbation.

"You really are just numb, aren't you?" Gerald says.

Mickey had read the first version of this silently when I met with her at Saddle Up Espresso. "Now, do you see what I mean, Mickey?" She responds: "I'm sorry," and her head drops slightly toward her chest. She sighs. "But it still isn't clear that oral sex explains what stands in your way to having a positive relationship." I am crestfallen. How can there be anything more compelling than the pain of that moment? Perhaps Mickey is just wrong.

* * *

I settle back into my seat in a cafe I'd found near the station and pull out a book I'd bought at a used bookstore for $1, a tiny little paperback titled *The Teachings of the Compassionate Buddha*. I scan the table of contents for a chapter I had been intending to read, "What is Gained by Abandoning the World and Becoming a Monk?" I have thought many times about becoming a Buddhist nun. But the paradox has always arisen in my mind:

If a woman becomes a nun when the sex drive is still there and she simply achieves celibacy, it will give the achieving practitioner a bigger ego. This comes from the pride she has, related to her success in refraining from sex. And ego is the very thing I wish to reduce, eventually obliterate, in my zen practice! That is, egolessness is the goal, right? Recognizing that possibility, of just getting a *bigger ego*, I've always given up the nun idea. Not to mention, I am really unlikely to carry out that celibacy. Even though sex hasn't been that great, one keeps trying, you know?

I read desperately for a way to escape. A practitioner frees her heart from lust. A practitioner becomes self-possessed. She becomes free, joyful, "and being thus at ease she is filled with a sense of peace, and in that peace her heart is stayed..." I go to a nearby park and sit in the half-lotus posture under a palm tree and meditate. Perhaps I've known all along how to escape samsaric relationships—it is just that my mind is prone to unpredictable flitting that betrays my goal of self-possession. I forget that I can meditate. Jesus! How is it possible to be so forgetful, trudging along in seeming oblivion?

Dear Katie,

I read that "iron and soul" chapter you sent me. And I thought that first chapter on how Gerald treated you was sad! My god! Why on earth would you stay with him? (I hope that doesn't overstep my bounds.) It is just hard to understand. I will try to write more later. A little rushed as I am waiting for a ferry to Iki Island and I notice folks are dashing out there now to catch it.
Best,
Steve

Dear Steve,

*I guess it would be hard to understand why I stay with Gerald. I'm sure it's because my vignettes are not completely fair. As they say, there are always two sides (or **many** sides) to the story. Actually, when I confronted Gerald about why he broke up with me because of lack of oral sex, he said that it wasn't that he was demanding a particular kind of sex, it was just that I had once seemed quite okay with it. Then, I had not only refused him oral sex but any kind of sex whatsoever. He said he was actually reacting to that and it had really hurt his feelings, made him feel like I didn't care for him any longer. So you see that he did have a point. It's odd how I didn't even remember his side of the story when I was writing it down. Shows how self-serving our memory can be, sometimes! In any case, thanks for reading the chapter.*
Best,
Katie

114

19 Out of the Frying Pan Into the Fire

Aggravation, also render worse, so much the worse, from bad to worse: 835, Roget's Thesaurus, 1947.

Thou shalt never forget the sixth commandment, Thou shalt never give up.

1935, Bud, Jesup, Georgia on the way to Florida. I left my usual route, hoping I could catch up to Harry again, who had carefully left a message on a water tower in Chicago that he had gone south, towards Florida. From the boxcar, I saw rambling kudzu vines, worn wagon paths that must've dated back to civil war times, and that veered off into nowhere when they curved into a heavy thicket.

I aimed to step off the train at the edge of the yard we was coming to, as soon as it slowed enough. Thank god for the end of the line. I smiled. But the air was too still. I strained to hear something. I shook my stiff shoulders after the long ride. But something made me uneasy. Too quiet. I began to sweat for no reason.

Felt like something was brushing against my neck. I slapped at my neck with my hat. Nothing unusual in the yard. *Still something, something just...*

Now a sound. The crunch of gravel. From the corner of my eye I saw a whip, an angry face. Coming, like a blur. Now it's right in front of me. *Too late.*

A bull jumped onto the boxcar and a whip seared into me. Hand over hand I scrambled for the other side of the boxcar. Maneuvered between two leaping cars. I was met on the other side by another face, a whip. I rolled to the ground and tried to protect my face. The whip reached through my shirt and left a welt under my rib. I felt the toe of a boot go into my other rib. *Too late. Too late to run. I'm gonna die...*

Instead, one of the bulls stepped forward and said, "Let me have him!" This bull drug me to my feet and told me I could cool my heels for awhile in the local jail. It turned out that he got a couple of dollars for every 'bo he brought in, alive.

Strange memory came on me then, considerin' the danger. I remembered Pa's gray eyes, and the smell of chewing tobacco, kinda sweet smell, and the rough feeling of his suspenders against my back, when he had held me. Must've been a tiny boy, 'cause he held me on his lap. That memory right then didn't help neither, 'cause you can't lose concentration if you wanna live.

Thrown into that cell in Jesup, my hands were shaking and my legs a'trembling. I was tired and it felt different from other times I'd been picked up. I didn't have the confidence that I could make it out. I just laid there, without much fight. That scared me more than the whips had. So this is how a man ends, I thought. Stuck in jail, alone with his regrets, abandoned and down on all fours. I checked my pockets. All the cash gone. My shoes off, socks too. "Son of a bitch, they got the money there, too. Money for a ranch gone."

I collapsed face up onto the cement floor, a small piece of cardboard between me and the cold. I looked up at the crumbling cement, florescence and water line stains. Figgered the cell walls had been flooded at one time. I twisted my neck around until I had taken in all four walls of the cell. Prisoners drowned here, either in their own blood, after being worked over by the bulls, and too sick and weak to turn over, or from a rush of water from the nearby gully, filling and swamping the cell. Everywhere was a dull pain and ache from the kicked ribs and the welts on my back. Flat on my back, I willed myself to turn over, lest the little gurgle of blood choked off my breathing. It warn't from my lungs. Just from a bloodied nose draining into my throat.

I wasn't sure I deserved to live. So this is how it goes. You might try your best but you are going to do something that you regret. Even thinking about getting the money back for the other 'bos wasn't working this time. I felt like sleeping. Even if it meant death.

Once the bulls left, I surveyed the damage. Welts front and back. Bruises from the boot. Clothes shredded... I didn't believe I'd survive a stint in this jail. But I still didn't have the energy to move. Evening by now, all of the bulls went home, leaving me with a pale brew of tea that they called soup. In some ways, death seemed better than living on the road, never at peace, going on and on, subject to the whip.

I drifted off, but startled awake by a barking dog. My mind wandered, and a faint light of wanting to live came in. It mingled with anger: I ain't gonna let them crush me the way I saw them crush them other guys, so that you couldn't see no freedom in them. I can't let that happen. I'd rather die. Ain't nothing worse for a man than that crushing out of his life until he's got no freedom. Can't move this way or that cause everywhere he turns, they've got some other scheme for stopping a man and taking everything he's worked for. Crushing us down to nothing. I'd rather die.

I'll work. I'll get the money again.

Disjointed thoughts roared through my worn out brain, and it was difficult to distinguish between the ache of a bruised body and the ache of being alone and going on. I knowed I'd have to fight to keep out of a cage. A life for a life, it says in the Bible. And it says "Thou shalt not kill." So how does a man avoid taking a life? Should a man give up his freedom? His own life? Some would say it was self defense. But I'm not sure. Are we just like animals? Fighting for territory and scraps. We ain't bad. Even those of us that stole had good reason. Well, most of us. There's a few that used the times for an excuse.

But, no, most of us didn't want to hurt no one. We ain't animals. We didn't have much choice. Well, I guess there's always some kinda choice. Could'a starved. Could'a been weak in the head, gone from pillar to post. Could'a laid down and died. But fighting was no good either. It sickens a man when someone dies at his hand. Ain't no cure for that sickness. The man is dead and you done it. The memory don't go away and you can still feel the nausea if the mind wanders. You can't unring that bell. Best thing. Pretend it never happened. Never tell anyone.

I drifted off again, maybe for five minutes, maybe for an hour, not sure. But it was still light and some source of strength pushed me to pull myself up off the floor, even though my body felt like lead. I stood for awhile, leaning against the cell wall.

If I live through this one, maybe I can settle. Contribute something to society. It will be a productive ranch and I'll have a family. Isn't that enough from a man? With these thoughts the energy came. And I began thinking. Even got clever.

I'd seen a young boy glancing at the barred window. "Hey," I called out. The boy came out of the bushes and slipped over to the jail window. He looked pretty rough, most likely been on the rails himself. "Look, here, if you can bring me a crowbar I can pry my way outta here. I don't have nothing now, but if I get out and can get to the next job, I'll help ya out." Much to my surprise, the boy showed up an hour later with a crowbar.

I set to work on the bars in the darkness. I was kinda scrawny then so I wouldn't have to pry them too far apart. Fortunately, they weren't that strong, and slipped apart with the crumbling cement. I crawled through the opening, and almost cried out when the kid tapped me on the shoulder. We kept quiet as we hightailed it to a jungle to find the first freight out.

"There better be one tonight," I whispered to the boy, "or we'll have to hike on outta here."

Once we found the jungle, we got the information we needed. We didn't have much time—it was the 10:10, and it didn't linger in the station beyond a few minutes. I knew the kid would slow me down, but a deal is a deal. I kept one eye out behind me as I made my way, the kid following close behind, for the yard. We crawled up close, still hidden by brush. As the train slowed to roll through the station, I nodded my plan to the kid. I motioned forward. We couldn't get on the train at its stop. Too risky. We gonna have to run alongside as it pulls out. The searches would have already been done, and with any luck they won't be looking this far up; they wouldn't believe someone would take that kind of leap onto a train, anyway.

Building up speed, the train approached. "Now," I shouted, not able to look back. I burst out of the undergrowth and got hold of the railing on the third car back. Once latched on I glanced around and to my surprise, the kid was grinning, hanging onto the railing of the next car back. It reminded me of myself, when I was going on fourteen and just started riding the rails. I began climbing to the top of the car because I saw that it had an opening and knew we could never hang on the way we were without being seen. I motioned upward, and we both began to inch our way forward and up. I reached the hole first, lifted the lid and dropped down. The kid was right behind me.

We both lay for a minute in the gloom, then discovered that there were two more men in the corner, laying out on some cardboard. The usual short greetings don't happen because we was too close to the conductor and don't want to be heard. All four of us bedded down and rode on out of Jesup. When the train was up to speed and making its usual noise, we was able to talk. I didn't know the yards this far south and needed to find out how to get through them and back up to Chicago.

"You'll have to ride it out for fifteen hours. They won't be bothering with inspecting these cars. Mostly they will be vagging the new ones trying to come on the train." Could we survive without water that long? I had a small flask, which I immediately offered to share.

Fortunately, the two men were prepared. I would only have to share my water with the kid. "Okay. So what's yer name? You don't look like you've been out long but the way you decked that car back there made it seem like ya had. And shh...keep it down."

"Name's Bailey," the boy said. "Figured I'd be better off getting out of that town with someone else. They was about to call in the authorities for underage boys, send me back to my Pa. He would'a killed me. That is, if the bulls didn't. Thought my chances was better this way."

"Well, seems like ya do have the luck of the Irish. And are mighty fast on yer feet." Both me and Bailey chuckled at that. I stopped laughing quickly, because my bruises were fresh and the belly jiggling hurt. Now the ache come on full force. I leaned back careful-like against the wall of the car and looked down at my feet. It was the first time I'd decked a train with no shoes and my feet was bleeding. I tore off a bit of sleeve and wrapped the worst of it.

As it turns out Bailey was a godsend. He helped me regain some of my cheeriness. He warn't with me fer long, though, and got a job on a place. I was happy I could help him get into a family situation as a long-term hand, by posing as his uncle.

It wasn't until I passed through Chicago, then reached New York, the bruises still visible but not as tender, that I caught up with Harry. And then it was pure chance, because we had agreed to meet around Tampa where Harry had planned to stay awhile and do some organizing.

20 A' Daniel Come to Judgment

Judge, also judicial, his worship: 967,
Roget's Thesaurus, 1947.

The seventh commandment broken, Thou shalt keep steady one's roots.

2009, Katie, continued layover in Los Angeles. I run my fingers over the rich embroidery on a blouse. Wandering down Pico Rivera Street, an open market near the train station with booth after booth of knock-off leather goods, pottery, tourist items, hats, shawls, peasant blouses, I can smell the leather shop next door. Its distinct odor mingles with the BBQ just across the way. Enjoying the colors and the sensuous goods, my senses heightened in the sun-drenched market, my mind wanders. This often happens. Just when I am beginning to feel happy, I'm brought down by a tough-to-digest memory, as if driven to keep the wound green.

* * *

"I want you to leave," I'd said. My voice shook.

"Why?" Wayne sounded shocked.

"I wanna be a family, do things together..." I trailed off, a buzz in my forehead, a lump in my throat. I looked over at the metal recipe box I'd been given by my mother. I'd put in 6x8 index cards, each with a suggestion for a

121

family outing. "Go on a picnic on the beach" is printed neatly on one of the cards. "Visit the La Brea Tar Pits" on another. I had filled out twenty cards, each with a different family activity.

Wayne turned away in disgust, or was it anger? when I show him the box. His betrayal of family caused burning tears to rise...and be refused. I willed myself to not cry.

As we unravelled we tried to talk. He denied that he drank too much. He made promises. He promised to help with the dishes. He said he would come home after work instead of stopping off at the bar.

It took weeks before I could bring myself to call my parents and tell them we had separated, knowing how dear they held family and family roots. When I did call they shocked me by saying, "Well, it's about time. We never thought he treated you that well."

* * *

Los Angeles, where I lived with Wayne and where I divorced Wayne. It was amazingly quick, too, with the judge stamping *final* on the pages within minutes of the beginning of the procedure. I find another open air cafe' on Pico Rivera street and sit down, order coffee.

Back to the present. I rise slowly and look at my watch to see how long I have before the train leaves. I haven't drunk my coffee, too distracted by the rush of memory and jotting it down. But I am too nervous to stay, order another one (this one too cold) or get food. So I pay at the counter and wander back towards the train station, head pounding and shoulders tense.

There is a reason I don't want to write about this. The memory leaves me anxious and at odds with myself. There are many memories we could just leave well enough alone. Perhaps toss them down an old, unused well and seal it up. That was the general rule in the Nolan family. Give up that wound. Don't let it go green. Let it alone. Get on with it. "Thank god," I say to no one, "Amtrak will leave in twenty minutes, and I can get back into the rhythm of the swaying train." At the station, my cell phone doesn't work so I dash into an old-fashioned phone booth and call Mickey.

"Where are you?" I hear faintly on the other end of a buzzing line.

"I'm in the L.A. train station. I have fifteen minutes before my train leaves. I just wanted to let you know I think I'm making progress."

"I'm sure you are. You need to have confidence." I can hear the encouragement in Mickey's voice.

"Well, it seems clear to me now that I have managed to choose emotionally distant men, drinking men. And a man who is a drunk cannot dream of a positive future for himself, let alone share my dreams. It has made for a lonely love life." Mickey is silent for a moment.

"Hmm...okay...that is an insight. Some women do have a pattern of dating and marrying alcoholics. You might want to explore more about the emotional distance. Is there something else? You seem to be pushing away some childhood memory—at least that is what you have hinted. Might that memory be a clue that is related to what you just told me?"

"Not at all," I assured Mickey. She was referring to one of my worst childhood memories, one that I'm pretty sure has nothing to do with relationships. If anything, it's related to my fear of heights. "That isn't worth dredging up," I assure her. "And some memories just shouldn't be dug up," I'd added.

Dear Katie,

It's nice to see an email from you. You'll be surprised by this, but I've actually had a similar experience to the one you've had with Gerald. I know. I know. Not the usual thing, as women are supposedly the sensitive ones and men the louts. But a woman actually sent me into this whole zen enterprise. Seeking I knew not what.

Since then, I studied for five years with a zen master in Seattle, Roshi Matsumoto, and have gotten a better idea of what it all meant. He's encouraged me to continue my practice, and thought that my visit to Japan would be significant. I hope I do not let him down, or myself, either.

Would you like to share more of your writing? And vice versa?

Yours,
Steve

Dear Steve,

Okay, but I am pretty distracted on this "hobo" trip, trying to digest the locations that my father had been in. Not sure how long we will be able to share, but sure, a few times of exchange might be fruitful.
K

I am intrigued by Steve but wary. He's probably a closet alcoholic. And, all caught up in zen? That could be okay, but some of the men I've met in zen monasteries are pretty sexist. I know this is sexist, but really? A guy who put up with bad sex? What's up with that? And I can't believe I shared that stuff with him about Gerald! My god, that was a bit much. I hope my email put him off in a polite enough way.

Dear Katie,

I have been thinking more about why we stay with lovers who keep their emotional distance. Common issue, I know, for someone to be hurt, then throw up defenses. I know I sure did and it was related to early loss of my father. Perhaps that doesn't sound all that dramatic, but it is my pain, and I've had to deal with it. Writing has helped. By the way, I don't know how you manage to do so much writing on the train! I think I would get too caught up in the scenes rolling by. But enough about therapeutic issues and writing!

Before I came to Japan, I often spent the day immersed in building a cabin on my property near Quilcene. I love the ideas about hand-built homes, self-sufficiency, and an eco-conscious lifestyle. And it is during building that I've often gotten insights into notions such as emotional distance, etc
Yours,
Steve

Wow, this guy isn't put off easily! I'll answer his email to be polite, but then...

124

Dear Steve,

It's great that you are trying an eco-conscious life, a life of simplicity. It seems to fit with your interest in zen. As a matter of fact, simplicity has always appealed to me, as far back as when I was a teen. I then imagined myself living in a hut in a developing country, saving people. It seemed so romantic! I do know better now, how the idea of being a savior is terribly colonialist, but I was naive then. Now, I just want to follow the ideas of the simplicity movement for its own sake, and its contribution to the environment. Hope your zen study is going well.

I do like writing on the train. I don't get too distracted by the scenery. Rather it seems to evoke memories from my past. But in the process, I do often forget where I am!

Yours,

K

21 Neither Fish Flesh nor Fowl nor Good Red Herring

Unconformity, non-conformist, also infraction, individuality, lawless: 83,
Roget's Thesaurus, 1947.

1935, Bud, New York Central Park, then, heading to Tampa again. A
voice booms: "Many of you have been shot at, beaten by the railroad bulls,
maybe even been on a chain gang. That isn't right. You have been denied
your rights. You work so why is it that you aren't making a living? Why aren't
you settling down right now on your own place with a wife and kids? It's the
system! They don't care what happens to you. No matter how hard you work
the system will abandon you without a second thought."

I heard the commotion and drifted over. A Communist Party leader
stood on a soapbox on a corner of New York's Central Park. It was
William Z. Foster.

The *system.* I noted Foster's emphasis on the word and waited to hear
more. The system? I was puzzled at that. But the guy went on to explain:

"It is a system where they get rich off your labor and give you next
to nothing. It is a system where they offer one guy a job at 25 cents an hour
and the next guy who's starving comes along and says he'll do it for twenty.
That's the way they like it." My ears perked up. I'd heard this before, and so
had many of the other men. We knew it was true. Foster continued: "It is a
system where they lock you up, or even kill the ones of you they don't want.
They say you are suffering because of the Depression. Yet, Carnegie says he'd
rather kill each and every one of you rather than give a single person a raise.
Kill you! Then, they wonder why you get forced into a corner sometimes and

126

kill one of them or one of their lackeys! Why, you got no choice! There ain't no criminals, like they say there are. They are the real criminals. You just do what you have to do! While Carnegie and others get rich off ya. Come to a meeting tonight, friends. We are the Communist Party U.S.A. The system has abandoned you. It is time for you to fight the system. Learn your rights."

I knew I was not going to a meeting. I stayed away from organized things like that. Figgered it was just another way to trap you, take away your freedom. But I felt dizzy upon hearing the other words. A system? I always figgered something was wrong with me. I made wrong choices. Well, maybe I did, but a system? Am I decent like the guy says? And that statement about working for twenty-five cents. I'd heard Harry say the same thing. If only I had someone to talk to. Then I heard a familiar voice.

"Hey, you old 'bo! What you doing here? I didn't know you'd gone communist." Harry smiled as he sauntered up.

"Well, I'll be damned," I said. "They haven't got ya yet. Been lookin' for you since we got separated in Chicago. Heard about some fool hightailing it from a pool hall. Knew that must be you."

"Humph."

"Let's go. Let's hit a jungle."

Harry and I found a camp on the East River. It stunk from the brackish, polluted water. We settled into the empty jungle, its old tents, upturned wooden boxes, and fire pit in the center like any other camp. We grabbed two boxes and shared bread.

"I need to settle down," I told Harry, and the emotion in my voice caught me by surprise.

"I reckon we both do."

"It's been seven years. And Harry," I said, "we was forced into things by the system..." I really wanted to hear Harry's agreement but the waiting was making me nervous.

"System, huh? Well, yeah. That's what I've been trying to say all along. I mean if we hadn't done what we did we would be dead. You know that. They was killing us one by one. The system didn't care. Just got replacements from more vagrants once we was dead. That's how the system works."

"Yeah, well how did we know it was gonna be us next...?" This is what had nagged me, caused me to doubt myself.

127

"Oh, we knew. You know, you regret something when you feel that you didn't make the right choice. But were you really free to make that choice? See, regret is related to losing freedom. Not just the freedom from jail, but the freedom we gotta have in our being. Freedom to make choices. But sometimes there ain't no choice. And then you do something that you regret. It isn't like you really make a decision about it. Just the urge comes on you, put there when you ain't' got no real choice, and you have to do it. Is a man on the road free to leave the rails anytime he wants, to settle down? Not when there ain't no jobs. He has to keep moving to find another job. When there ain't no choice there ain't no freedom. This fear of losing freedom keeps us apart, though, makes for loneliness. Always fearing you're gonna lose your freedom makes you want to steer clear of others." Harry sat back and put both hands on top of his head and rubbed it, making his straw blonde hair look like a small haystack.

"Well, looks like I didn't quite manage to steer clear of you." I grinned at him then, trying to lighten things up.

"Guess not. Here we are." Harry grinned back. But then he sobered and went on: "Well, you know, we sometimes begin to doubt ourselves. Doubt is worse than fear, though, because when we doubt ourselves we can't move forward. We have to let fear and doubt go to be free. We've got to be moving, choosing, and changing to be alive! To be free! But of the two, fear and doubt, doubt is the worst."

I only half understood Harry's philosophizing, but it was his certainty that got to me and my eyes went moist. I had been afraid, but I had always been able to talk myself out of fear, to leave it behind with action. But doubt. Doubt had stopped me in my tracks. I knew I had too much doubt to do what Harry did—all that organizing for the Wobblies. Harry seemed to have answers. All I had was questions.

Harry noticed me struggling with myself and looked away out of respect.

Then, I crumpled over, trembling some.

Harry awkwardly laid his arm across my shoulders and we sat that way, on the edge of the jungle, while I still had the shakes, until we heard the noise of a few men coming down the trail. We abruptly sat up stiff and

128

straight. We sat silent and I continued a'clearing my throat and a'swallowing. Then, I got hold of m'self and broke the silence.

"I'm gonna do it," I said. "In spite of 'em. I'm gonna get that ranch and settle down."

"Me, too." Harry grinned. Embarrassment was there between us, we both having loyalty welling up.

I grabbed a bucket and headed for the river. Smelly water be damned, I thought, I'm gonna bathe. I went up the path part way and stripped down.

"Hey," Harry called out. "I'm joining ya."

I noticed Harry's white belly and legs, in sharp contrast to his tanned chest and back.

I looked down and saw that I looked just as ridiculous. My chest hair was a lot thicker and darker than Harry's, which was blonde and a bit wispy. A chill in the air, I shivered. We both got the same idea. Harry got there first, grabbed the bucket, and chased me down the trail, dousing me from the back. I grabbed for him, catching his arm, and twisting him to the ground. In a quick turn, I filled the bucket from the river behind me and poured it over Harry's head.

"Yep. Looks like you're almost baptized, and you need it in the worst way—eeyew, smelly old 'bo. You reek worse than a polecat!" I said.

"You're the worst. You smell like two polecats trapped under a porch by a hound dog!" Harry said, and leaped up and grabbed the bucket and went after me. Taller than me, Harry's long legs made him awkward. We both went down and rolled down the trail, the bucket tumbling into the shallow of the river, as we busted up laughing.

In a few days we beat our way down to Tampa, where Harry had some unfinished business.

"So, what you got goin' that has got us back south again?" Me and Harry sat on boxes in a Tampa jungle and was basking in the warm evening.

"They actually use the police to get workers around here," Harry said. "Not only that, but out a ways from Turkey Creek I found out that they worked us all on this railroad grading outfit as if it was a prison farm. On our monthly pay day we found out that practically all of us were in debt to the contractor.

129

Just like in the prison camps, they charged us with a variety of things at high prices, and these things were checked off against our wages of eighty cents a day. Only a few had any money coming. There was lots of grumbling but when I asked the men to strike they were just too badly demoralized to take a stand. And if anyone quit, by the time they reached Turkey Creek the police vagged 'em and they were forced onto the Florida chain gangs."

"So, what ya think you can do?"

"I promised this young guy, good guy, with a wife and kids up in Georgia, that I'd be back to help him get out. A donkey engine fireman, so his wage was a dollar a day, and he had twenty-one days of pay coming. But after three weeks of hard work, he was six dollars in debt. He was scared to 'blow' because of the threat of the chain gang, and he wanted to get back to his family. Would like to get 'em all out but that would be too dangerous."

"Hell, Harry, sounds like trouble!" I looked at Harry, grinning when I said it.

"Sure as hell is," Harry responded. Then we both fell silent thinking about how to get the guy out.

"Here's the plan. Get a message to the guy, Tom's his name, that he needs to do something, anything, to delay going out to the works. Then, when he does head out they'll direct him to get on down the road. There's a fork in the road that's out of sight. So where he should turn right, he should turn left instead. We'll be there waiting for him and we'll hot foot it back to Turkey Creek. If his delay story works, they won't check on him until we are long gone."

"But how we gonna get a message to him?" I looked at Harry, shaking my head a little at his crazy plan.

"The guys go into the company store a quarter mile from camp. We will drift in with them, find him and hand him a note. He's expecting something from me so he hopefully won't wince. Really short guy, shorter than you, maybe five foot four, so's he'll be easy to pick out. Got red hair, skinny."

"Okay. But I got to hand it to you, Harry. You're gonna get rid of these pe'onage camps one worker at a time." I had emphasized the word peonage, and exaggerated the accent on the first syllable, having learned the word from Harry, and wanting Harry to be impressed.

"Well, a man's gotta keep his word," Harry said.

130

"We'll likely all end up on a chain gang if we get caught." I took a deep breath. "We can't get caught..."

Me and Harry arrived at the right time for blending in with the workers on their walk to the store. We slipped out onto the road from a thicket, and since there were twenty or more guys, we blended in. The other workers assumed we were new hires.

Harry strode into the store, while I waited on the porch, watching for trouble. Harry got the note to Tom, and then me and Harry waited around until a little group started back. We lagged behind and slipped out of sight, taking to the thicket again.

"What, now?" I whispered.

"We wait 'til morning."

We bedded down in the thicket near the fork where Tom would be heading, if the plan worked.

It was a long night and I laid awake thinking about the workers' situation. Why if we work hard, they rob us. And if we are minding our own business trying to get to the next job, they try to put us in some prison camp or on one of their chain gangs. I began to try to think of a way out for myself and for all of us. From my spot on the ground, I glanced over at Harry. That is the kind of guy you don't meet often, thinking about others when his own lot ain't good. A good guy, a really good guy.

Unbelievably, Tom showed up around nine the next morning. He'd feigned illness, stuck his finger in his throat and vomited, and bought some time, then followed Harry's instructions perfectly. The three of us moved silently down the road, avoided taking any chances, moved as fast as we could on foot. In a few hours we made it to the freight yard and decked the first freight north. Tom had managed to slip some tobacco into his pocket and he passed it to Harry along with some papers. We leaned back against the metal of the boxcar, hearts still pounding, like men's hearts pound who come near death.

Tom started to speak, to thank Harry. Instead he made a strange coughing sound. Harry knew what he wanted to say. It didn't need to be expressed.

I looked at Harry. "Well, you sure know how to get us about killed. Can't think what I'd do without ya."

We all started laughing. Then, words came tumbling out of all of us. Hell of a thing they got going for themselves. Yeah, the bastards. So-called free labor is about as free as a prison. Well, they ain't gonna get away with it forever. I heard that they was going to crack down on 'em. Saw it in a newspaper. Anyways, we are the lucky ones. Those poor suckers that was left behind. And the conversation rambled until we saw our rescuee off "way up north in Georgia" where he'd come from.

22 Whether One Stands on One's Head or One's Heels

Uncertainty, also blind bargain, addle the wits, flounder: 475,
Roget's Thesaurus, 1947.

*There is nothing more dreadful than the habit of doubt. Doubt separates
people. It is a poison that disintegrates friendships and breaks up pleasant relations. It is a thorn that irritates and hurts; it is a sword that kills.*
—Buddha

*Thou shalt never forget the second Nolan commandment, Thou shalt keep it close
to your chest.*

**2009, Katie, leaving L.A. on the *Southwest Chief*, bound for Arizona and
New Mexico.**   I wake up to a view of the sandstone formations of Arizona,
and an incredible sunrise of yellow and orange, so dazzling it takes my breath
away. Many have remarked upon the sculptural nature of these orange behe-
moths, some rising smoothly and rounded off at the top and others twisted
in fascinating shapes. This route is the Southwest Chief that crosses into New
Mexico going towards Albuquerque. I luxuriate in the swaying bed, having
splurged and taken a sleeper for the night.

I look around the sleeper car, trying to pull myself into the present. I
look out the window. It helps to watch the sunrise until I get hungry. I pull
the tiny metal door of the closet open, drag my jeans and a black T-shirt off
the hangers, then dress hurriedly and head for the snack car, groaning silently when I remember I'd promised myself last night that I would address my
failed loved story, once and for all, really!

But first I am going to grab coffee and a breakfast sandwich and enjoy
it in the lounge car. It's fairly empty this early in the morning. I finish breakfast and jot down notes. I will get rid of this confusion!

I still can't clarify all the connections to gain an insight into my failure at love, but I am getting the hint that it is not only about my heroic father (that no man could match up to), and often drunk husbands and boyfriends. I look back through my journal notes to see what else I've explored as possible connections, making a list:

Can't relate to Gerald because of class differences.

Can't relate because I am just too opinionated.

Can't relate because I can't do oral sex, the thing men want most.

Can't relate because I can't ask for what I want.

Can't relate because of my overwhelming lack of trust (that's like doubting everyone and everything they say!)

Can't relate because I choose men who are heavy drinkers or alcoholics.

Why hasn't Mickey accepted any of these as the answer to What's at stake? She says I'm making progress through the process of elimination, so that's good. And she does agree that any one of these issues can contribute...

Mickey keeps asking me to write about childhood trauma. I didn't really have a terrible childhood, I assure her. But I do realize she is right when she points out that I haven't written anything about my second husband. I sigh, recalling how we separated.

* * *

Poor Jerry! Husband number two. He looked a bit stunned.
"You're going to Japan?" he said, frowning.
"Yes, but just for one year." I felt guilty but I didn't make a clean break. I didn't tell him I was *actually* leaving him. In fact, to keep up the

pretense, I told him that I planned to send him a few hundred dollars a month from Japan to help him with his law school tuition. And, I promised to call him regularly.

The deal breaker: Once I was in Japan, he tells me I needn't bother to call for a few months. I felt abandoned again. Because he was the one who first moved out from our shared home. My teen-aged son took Jerry's vintage car and ran it up a telephone pole. I understand that it's hard to take on a ready-made family, but where was his commitment?

I'd doubted Jerry before, but I thoroughly mistrusted him after he moved out at the least hint of trouble. This was not to be the only time he abandoned me. He convinced me to take a job in a group home for autistic young adults in Alaska. When that became difficult, off he went, leaving me there to fend for myself. So, I felt justified in going off to Japan. Eventually, he surprised me by following me there.

Oh, my, what a disaster! One evening, while sitting uncomfortably across from me at the kotatsu, he sincerely asked me what I needed to be satisfied. This was a first. Back home, we had gone months without sex. And he had ignored the book I had strategically placed on the bedside stand, *The Joy of Sex.*

Later, I responded by pulling his fingers down my loose pajama bottoms and splaying them across my clitoris, moving them just right, until I had an orgasm. We then lay side by side on our backs on the futon laid out on the tatami mats. The awkward silence yawned between us.
That taught me something. A lover giving you an orgasm without much enthusiasm on their part leaves one hollow.

* * *

Back in my seat, I cringe at the memory of Jerry, the train rocking comfortably down the tracks. I fall asleep. An announcer's voice. "Next stop is Albuquerque." The loudspeaker voice encroaches on my state between sleep and wake. I sit up, swaying forward with the stop.

I cannot write for two days, staring out at landscapes, eating meals for a welcome distraction, glancing hopefully at my laptop from time to time.

135

Finally, I decide I can write and will write about my father. Maybe that will help make that long list of possible connections make sense. Maybe I can begin to make sense of why I doubt everything and everyone.

Did I become overwhelmed with lack of trust because of genetic memory? Did I inherit my father's distrust?

Dad never talked about his relationships with me. I have just had to imagine them from bits and pieces I'd learnt from other family members, including my mother. From hearing about the women through family gossip, I began to see that at one time my father tried to establish enough trust to gain intimacy.

Occasionally, my mother described her early dating of my father as very romantic. Her and her best friend Vi (short for Viola) were maids in Portland and would go down to the lobby of a fancy downtown hotel, The Malloy, to wait for their dates—they couldn't afford to eat there but they liked watching all the people. And they sat there proud and straight- backed, dressed up and in high heels. "Then we walked all over Portland in them high heels, and that was a trial." I recall this statement by my Mom and smile at the image.

But there was always a rumor that my father once had a woman named Loretta, someone before Mom, and I'm pretty sure she never wore high heels.

Part Two

Fiddle-Faddle, Flapdoodle

23 Dear as the Apple of One's Eye

Love, also look sweet upon, take a fancy to: 897,
Roget's Thesaurus, 1947.

Thou shalt never forget the ninth commandment, Thou shalt get on with it.

1937, Bud, around Chicago. Me and Harry had separated again after our adventure in Florida, and after we had passed through Atlanta, then met briefly again in Chicago. It was safer that way. Over a year had passed since I'd seen Harry. I felt the loss of Harry as a kind of hunger. I longed to speak to a sympathetic human being. I hungered for trusted companionship, to stop feeling like a dog left off at the side of a road, continually loping forward, never likely to find his way home. That was when I met Loretta.

She had curly brown hair that poked helter skelter from beneath a worn beret. She was wearing a faded blue, man's shirt, its buttons angled toward her tiny waist because the shirt had been twisted before it was jammed into the waist band of her blue jeans. The jeans were too large on her making her look hungry.

Loretta was one of the few women who rode the rails, so I was surprised when I saw her. It wasn't safe for women because the other hobos tended to think the women who deck trains were prostitutes. Also, the bulls were vicious and would not only attack them, but also make them into sex slaves, put in jail cells where they were held separately, sometimes for years.

139

Some women risked it anyway, leaving a worse situation at home. Loretta had been tortured by her stepfather and the cigarette burn marks on her upper and lower arms were always carefully covered over by a long-sleeved shirt. She had also been kept on a chain gang by the guards, and repeatedly raped by all of them.

When I met Loretta, I had never seen such things, the burns, the guarded look in her eyes, and her way of flinching when anyone got close. My parents had beat me, yes, but it had always seemed fair, their effort to help me mature, even if maybe a little rough. What had been done to Loretta sent a chill up my spine. When I first caught sight of the scars, my eyes misted up. How can people do this to another human being? It was my first brush with evil of this type.

Me and Loretta jumped down from the boxcar. I don't want to see her go her own way, so I tried to strike up a conversation. I glanced down at my own pants and suddenly felt self-conscious about the oil stains on both knees of my overalls, about the tattered ends of the pant legs, which used to be cuffed.

"Hey, where you headed?" I paused awkwardly as soon as I'd said it. Likely she'd heard that way too much.

"No wheres," Loretta said flatly.

"I ain't, I don't..." I began to stutter.

"Well, say what you're gonna say!" Loretta looked at me a little more kindly.

"I can help, some," I said. I was hesitant.

"Okay," Loretta answered matter-of-factly.

"I got a small stash, could rent a little walk-up. Then, you could take a break from the road." I said this in a rush. It was a small thing I could do. Or maybe life would lose all meaning if I couldn't do this.

"That'd be nice," Loretta said.

Now, I kept stride with Loretta and she seemed to ease into having my company.

"I've been this way before. I know a room where they rent for a few weeks, no questions asked." I felt good that I could offer this. A break from running scared. I had often thought about landing there for a few weeks my-self, but I'd never done it.

"Okay, good. You lead the way." Loretta sounded a bit more relaxed now.

While Loretta stood below, I leapt up the stairs two at a time and someone opened a door. I came back out, holding a key. To Loretta's surprise I left her there in the walk-up, letting her know I was heading for the nearest jungle, but I'd be back.

Shortly after meeting Loretta, I fell into a singing gig. I wanted to earn a little money and continue helping Loretta out. It was similar to how I got started into everything else.

The opportunity came up. I was always ready to give things a try because ya never knew when it might work. This time the gig fell in my lap because Loretta knew the owner of the bar. I'd been thinking about trying to sing for my supper. "Can't know unless you take a look see," I often said, something I'd heard Pop say. It turns out that I sang off key but the storytell-ing in-between kept them laughing, and made up for that.

I was quite taken by Loretta, and I began thinking about how I could, maybe, settle down. I'd really given up on the idea, thinking no one would have me if they knew I was on the run. But maybe Loretta...

We spent an entire day together, taking a little road trip, picnicking on the beach at Lake Michigan. Loretta had on a green dress, a silky sash tied to one side. Her white legs were visible under the crepe, and I stared at her, her soft brown curls glinting in the sunlight. I began to ache for her and couldn't wait until we got back to the walk-up, to her bed. As we entered the room, Loretta wrapped her arms around my neck, and I began to cover her face and her arms, with kisses. She pulled me down on the bed. She was passionate, ready. I was a bit awkward because this was the first woman I had made love to (at least a woman who was not a prostitute). So I undressed her gently, but a bit rushed. I buried my face in her breasts, then kissed one then the other. "I'm ready, hon, ready." Loretta whispered in my ear.

I slid my hand into her panties, relieved that she was helping me know what got her ready, grateful that she was guiding my hand, showing me what pleased her. After making love, we both lay back, smiling, exhausted, elated. Then, I looked over at Loretta, my eyes gone a little soft.

"Loretta, have you thought about, maybe, having a family?"

"Why sure, honey. That would be a better life."

"I've been planning on getting some land. A few chickens. Some cows. Always gotta have some stock on the place to keep the pasture down. Maybe some pigs. Then, we'd have all the food we ever wanted. And there would be nobody telling us to move on. I'd build a little cabin at first, then, we could gradually expand it, when we needed more room."

"And I could collect the eggs," Loretta said. "Maybe get up a breakfast of pancakes, bacon, and eggs. That'd be nice."

"Sure would." I leaned back on my pillow and imagined how it would be. The room smelled of Loretta's perfume, labelled Paris and sitting on a shabby wooden bureau, along with the smell of cigarettes, and the musty smell of an old building, its inner walls water-stained in big half-circles at each of its corners. I stared up at the bare light bulb over the bed, then reached up, propping on one elbow, to pull the string to turn it off. I turned toward Loretta, whose back was toward me now, and draped my arm over her, pushing my chest as close as I could into her back, spooning into her. The bed made a strange noise, like the rattle of garbage being picked up, because it was propped on two corners by old paint cans.

I knew I'd have to find a better job than singing at a honky tonk if I was going to take care of Loretta, but I believed I could if I tried hard enough. Get enough money for the ranch, make it a good place for kids. Find some remote place where the authorities would never think to look.

Day after day I went around Chicago, looking for work. All I could come up with were two or three day jobs, washing dishes, busing tables, tending a coal furnace, and at night, cleaning up in a restaurant or a bar after hours. I wasn't about to give up. And if we have to go on the run together, well, I reasoned, at least it was better than what had happened to Loretta so far.

Months went by with me working for, and planning, our escape.
We began to live together, like husband and wife, although I was gone a lot,
trying to earn enough to carry out our dream.

I even got optimistic. I know folks I'd met thought I was cheery, but
before now that was just put on. We would make it out of this jam.
It was hard to leave Loretta when I went to work and I got excited when the
end of shift came, her smile, her heart-shaped face, with two pin curls on the
sides framing it, flashing up in my mind as I rushed to get to her.

I finished cleaning up in a bar around three in the morning, and decided to drop by to see Loretta on my hour break between jobs. Even though
I hadn't slept much in days, I was full up with energy because I had stashed
fifty bucks away. Soon, I could leave with Loretta for something better.

Since the walk-up had a window facing the street, I would be able to
see if she was up. Excited, I approached and was thinking about how I would
share some of my dreams. I bound up the steps after seeing the light. I was
also looking forward to the comfort I felt when we were holding each other
and talking. Just as I got to her door, I stopped short. Loretta was with someone and she was giggling. Then, I heard a man's voice.

"You're the best there is, you know."

Then, silence except for the rattle of the bed on the cans, and more
giggling from Loretta.

It turned out that the woman I loved didn't love me, or if she did,
well, I thought, she's got a funny way of showing it. I felt a twinge in my gut,
first time a woman made me feel something like that, then blackness, as if the
world had slipped away, then I caught myself, fought myself back. I'd let no
one have this kind of power over me. I stiffened my back, turned, and walked
back down the stairs, slow-like, one step at a time.

The next day, I decked a train out of Chicago and didn't stop travelling until Los Angeles. Maybe there would be more steady work, and I began
to plan for it, anything, to distract myself. I had heard that the harvest work
is pretty good out there. My thoughts rushed. The rock of the train and the
familiarity of it helped, even though I felt a stab of loneliness come up under
my ribs, just like when I first left home.

Maybe that's when I learned to watch myself. Make sure a woman
didn't do me that way. Most likely explains why the next feller I saw asked me
why I was looking so grim.   143

24 Gathered to One's Fathers

Also, behind the veil, cross the Stygian ferry, peg out, hop the twig: 360, Roget's Thesaurus, 1947.

Thou shalt never forget the third commandment, Thou shalt never grieve.

1940, Bud, near Kansas City, not sure if in Kansas or Missouri. Next time I saw Harry, he was lying in the corner of a boxcar, a crude splint on his leg. It looked bad, black and rotted. "How'd it happen? An old 'bo like you?" I was trying to sound lighthearted but I knew he was in trouble.

"Must be getting old," Harry said. "Decked a train going a little faster than usual and didn't get a good grip. Finger nails was scraping across the wood floor, getting splinters, but I held on. Was okay until a bull wrapped his whip around one of my legs sticking out the car. Almost got ground under but fell off to the side. But went down hard and got the whip."

"Humph," I looked down at the plywood floor. The fear of the older 'bos. They might not be able to settle down, and they can lose their ability to deck trains, outrun bulls, or stay out of the way of local thugs having it in for 'bos.

Next stop, two of the older 'bos on that car helped get Harry to the hospital. We were ignored. When we began to insist, we were threatened with police.

"Let's move on," Harry said.

"We need to keep trying." One of the old 'bos spoke, matter-of-factly, keeping the worry out of his voice.

"No. No. I don't want to spend my last days dying in some jail. And they sure as hell would let me do just that, if they pick me up." Me and Harry exchanged glances. Both of us knew that if we were recognized, somehow, even though years had passed, we would likely both be in for life, or hung. If the police let us get that far. Hospitals were one of those places that men got picked up by cops.

There was nothing else we could do but make it to the nearest jungle, find out where we could deck a train, and do what we could ourselves, until we could try the hospital in the next town. We managed to slip onto a boxcar in the yard, one 'bo steadying Harry's leg, while the other two of us pulled him onto the car.

But as the boxcar lurched along, me and Harry both began to feel the resignation, like a heavy weight descending on the gut. Even if we made it to the next hospital, what were the odds that they would be more likely to treat Harry?

"Remember what ya said, Harry, that they'd just as soon see us die. Don't let 'em win this one. You ain't gonna die. We'll get you into the hospital next town. Just hang on..." I was getting choked a little on those last words, but held it back for Harry's sake.

"So, you agree with me after all this time, eh?" Harry managed to squeak this out, trying to sound strong. But he wasn't. His energy was ebbing away, and it was four hours to the next town with a hospital. Each minute stretched to an hour and the hours seemed like days. It still agitated me to think about this, and I just couldn't get a handle on why I hadn't been able to bring myself to throw in my lot with the Wobblies.

I broke the silence. "Harry, we didn't come this far to see you split yer head on a rock." I figgered I warn't successful in hiding that the cheerful delivery was false. I leaned Harry into my shoulder to cushion the bounce of the tracks. The other 'bos jumped off at the next small berg without a word. They might've given up hope but I hadn't. It was impossible to lose Harry. I'd get him somewheres for help.

Harry leaned on me and his breathing began to even. He relaxed some. "Hey, you know, we hoi polloi have grand plans that never come to fruition. We say, oh well, warn't meant to be." Harry didn't believe this was the end. We both held on.

"Harry, you're like kith and kin. We practically got blood ties that say we're too tough to die."

Harry smiled. "Reckon you're right." He shifted his good leg, bent it up to brace himself. The leg wobbled and I caught it and held it where he'd aimed it. Harry's breath was slowing, becoming weaker.

I was hating the bulls for the welts across his back. I was hating the bulls for my friend's broken leg. I was hating the people at the hospital in Kansas City that turned us away. My friend's leg gone.

Harry's hand grip on my forearm relaxed. I sat there for what might've been hours, staring at the landscape whizzing by, breathing shallow, glancing down at Harry now and then.

In my arms, Harry began to feel stiff. I gently lowered his eyelids. Then, I slumped back against the wall of the boxcar, Harry awkward across my lap. Harry 'n me had been together for ten years, at least. That's why I wept a little. At first it was dry heaves, then the tears flowed, dropped off the end of my jaw, dropped on Harry's face, dropped until I was wrung out and didn't care if I lived or died.

It was in this state I met up with Monte, Harry still slumped next to me. I was dried up but vowed to grieve no longer.

Monte had plans. He was gonna save up enough to start a junk yard. He had found out you could get a job in the sawmills, one that lasts awhile. All you had to do was get out West. Then, Monte was going to get married, settle down, have a home and a family.

I sat silently through all this chatter from Monte, nodding occasionally. Hours had passed since Harry'd stopped breathing and he was lying by my side now, draped over with a blanket.

"He okay?" Monte asked. Seemed he hadn't noticed someone was slumped beside me 'til now.

"No." Monte knew not to ask more questions. An unwritten law to spare another man's feelings.

146

I had to figure out what to do with Harry. I knew he was no longer in touch with any of his family. I didn't want the bulls to have him and carry him off to the coroner's, then the county. Harry deserved better than Potter's field.

So Monty and I spent a day, talking and digging, near the jungle and well hidden in a thicket. Harry was there, wrapped respectfully in my best blanket, one I'd taken with me from the bunkhouse at the Gregerson ranch. It was slow goin' cause the roots was thick. I cut them with my pocket knife as we dug. Occasionally, a big rock had to be levered out, which we did with strong branches from the cottonwoods, and whittled to a dull point on the ends. My thoughts roamed to the people I'd seen die. That 'bo down in Tampa that slipped and got ground under. That old 'bo that died from the bull's bullet...

I'll never get to ask Harry whether he thinks I'm a criminal. I know I asked him before, but I need to hear his answer again. Did we have to do what we did? Was there some other way to survive? I could answer these questions for myself, but not such that I could erase all doubt. I needed Harry for that. That was because I had faith in Harry's thinking.

I began wishing it were me, not Harry. This thought I tried to stuff as soon as it snuck up on me. It scared me. Then, I felt the same anger I'd felt when they jerked that guy who was dying in prison.

It rose like a hot wave. I stopped talking, not wanting to have the anger boil out of m' mouth. No one in their right mind would press me. Perhaps Monte sensed this, because he worked on silently for awhile, glancing at me now and then.

So, it wasn't until later, and after a campfire was built, that Monte broke the silence. "How 'bout you, Bud? Why'd you leave home? Your folks still around?"

I was hunched over on an old dynamite box, staring into the flames. I had been sitting like this for over an hour before Monte had joined me, thinking over my life, Harry's life, my thoughts settling in my gut like undigested food. Birds made their sounds, wind sighed, the fire crackled, but it was as if all of it was at a great distance, as if I was floating away into a void, the sounds a whisper. I wanted to go with Harry down into the earth. Only there, perhaps, I could take root. Start over again. Like a seed that has found its lonely way beneath the soil, almost drying up and succumbing to the darkness, then deciding to try again, given the slightest hint of moisture and warmth.

I responded, leaning back a little.

"Oh, I guess my mother'd taken to yelling 'til I couldn't take it no more. At first Pop came got us when we'd been vagged but after awhile he didn't have the energy. Got vagged himself a couple of times. I beat it for Chicago. Thought there would be more jobs in the big city. Weren't though. Had a heap of trouble riding the rails, too. Besides. Not much goin' on at home. Watery stew, lard gravy, or nothing but potatoes and corn, most all the livestock sold off trying to hold onto the place. Pop drinking more n' more and Mom just fussing."

Now, really warming up, as if my voice finally shifted into gear and was goin' on without me, I sat up straight on the box, my legs stretched out so's my feet pointed towards the fire, and I went on.

"Besides, I had just kicked the principal down the stairs, sick of him calling us little sons-of-bitches. Then, threatening to beat us if we was late. And we was, usually, after the chores was done, but that warn't none of his business. Never worked a day in his life, his lily-pink-fingers, the bastard! I got him good, though, kicked him clean to the landing before he could raise a hand. Well, anyway, it was a good time to get out. Didn't tell Mom, or nobody. Knew Mom would fuss."

All of this comes out at once. It was a relief to have someone listening. Felt like I was watching myself talk in slow motion from a distance. I wondered why it was I still wanted to live.

Monte had enthusiasm. He hadn't got caught up in the hatred or despair, even though he wore some of it on his face.

It had been a long day.

Monte nodded toward the river. "Look at them buds on that cherry over there."

"Yeah, mighty nice," I heard myself say.

We picked a few boughs and lay them on the grave, and in the soft light, with the fire flickering in the background, it had a certain grace, like folk art, or like a hymn sung enthusiastically in a country church.

148

The sun was goin' down and the flowers and fresh earth had a warm, sweet wetness.

Me and Monte had to get back to the jungle, find out the local information, maybe look up some food on the way.

At least the county hadn't got him. And Harry was buried in a damned purty place.

25 Wastrel

Traveller, also wanderer, gad-about, stray, vagabond: 268,
Roget's Thesaurus, 1947.

Thou shalt never forget the fourth commandment, Thou shalt always appear calm.

1940, Bud, Chicago. I was sitting on an old dynamite box and Monte was chopping vegetables. We'd set ourselves up in a Chicago jungle. Just when I was getting ready to lean back and stick both legs up on the stump nearby, two guys come into camp wearing uniforms. 'Bout then I stopped breathing and I was sittin' up straight. They flashed a badge all right. This is it, I thought.

"Heard that two guys buried somebody out near Kansas City. You guys know anything about that?"

"Nope." I heard Monte's sure tone. Figured I could match it. "Nope," I said.

"Well, he was an IWW red so good riddance. But he had a buddy and they got in some trouble awhile back. Let us know if you hear of some guy grieving over his buddy. There's a reward in it." They gave us their cards with a local address. Any one of the guys in camp could've been grieving over their buddy. I guess they looked over the lot of us and figgered they couldn't tell who was who. But they still stuck around awhile.

My throat constricted when I saw the handle of the shovel we used barely sticking out from the tent. I quickly looked away and I kept my eyes trained steady on what Monte was doing. They looked around some more, missed seeing the shovel, then left.

"Jeez, what was that all about. Can't a guy bury a friend without the cops botherin' them?" So that was all Monte said. No other questions asked. I figured I could trust Monte after that.

After a long silence, Monte speaks again. "Hey, I read in the newspaper that we wanna be homeless, gotta wander-bug. Whaddya think?" He asked me this as he stirred the big pot of mulligan's stew. I watched as Monte dipped to the bottom with the big slotted spoon. The potatoes rose to the top, then carrots, then onions. Someone had found some rosemary and it danced up to the surface with each stir. The smell of rosemary, like Mom used to have in her garden, and the cooking carrots was sweet, and my mouth began to water. Sometimes, the best part of the meal, smelling it before she's done. And this time the smell helped stop my churning stomach.

"Wander-bug?" I began to laugh a hearty belly laugh, roaring until my sides hurt. It set us both off laughing. We roar until tears are rolling down our faces, until heads turn, trying to figure out what's so funny. All one of us had to do was say the word again, *wander- bug*, or sometimes, *gad-about*, and we were off in renewed peals of laughter. Then, sobering up, I had something to say.

"They're getting us confused with the college boys hitching a ride."

"Yeah," Monte responded. "All's they gotta do is wire for some money if they get stuck. If we are outta money we gotta drink the cup of humiliation to the dregs, begging at a back door."

"You're a regular poet today." I looked over at Monte with a surprised smile. And it was funny to think of Monte getting mistaken for a college kid, with his squared jaw, and his long scar extending from his right ear to the shadow by his nose. I reckon I'm lucky with my scar running down my back—but still don't look like no college kid. No one asked Monte how he got that scar. No one dared.

We were both quiet now, reflecting on the fact that no one was likely to send us anything. In fact, we felt bad that we couldn't send something to our folks, to keep them from starving. After a long silence, I came back from my reveries, crouched down on m' haunches, beginning to relax after the scare.

"Reckon ya gotta make the best of it," I said.

"Whaddya mean?"

"If you go on worrying about when you're gonna get a job, when you're gonna get married, when things are gonna be better, you'll drive yourself crazier than a March hare. Better just enjoy the good parts of it and keep goin'. Help each other out, when ya can."

"Gonna get married yourself someday?" Monty asked.

"Yeah, sure. I'll settle down. Need a steadier job, though." I shoved my hat back, scratched my head to knock off the leaf that landed.

And that part about settling down. I tried to believe it was possible. But it was getting harder to imagine. A small, quiet voice had always had its say, "You're a fugitive. What you thinking. You ain't gonna be safe to settle." Now, with that little visit from the cops that voice was getting bigger and louder. Still, I knew what Monte had expected to hear and I wasn't gonna disappoint.

"How 'bout you, Monte, you aiming to settle down?"

"Someday." First time I laid eyes on Monte, I noticed he had the face of a lion but the heart of a deer. It was this that had impressed me, gave me the idea that maybe I could trust Monte. Also, Monte reminded me some of my youngest brother, Vic. Sort of quiet until you got to know him—then you might hear him roar. Monte also had that typical Irish, thin-lipped grin that lit up his face.

"Heard there's work out west, Washington, Oregon. Think I'll head out there," Monty said. Like Monty, I had been told there were more jobs out west, so Monty's plan made sense. It was the kind of thing hobos shared, where to get jobs, what towns to avoid because of hostile bulls, and where you could land a good meal. Once, when asked why we didn't stay on a job after we'd gotten enough to eat, so's we could save up, better our lot in life, we both answered: "It wouldn't feel right to take a job when somebody else really needed it. Not when they'd go hungry cause you took it."

"A feller really gotta help the other guy out," was something we'd hear a lot. And, "If you're hungry on the road, don't worry none 'bout ownership of fruit trees and bread. But never take what you don't need in case someone else needs it. A man's life is the important thing."

"Which freight's gonna take us outta here?" I asked.

"Track fourteen, in about an hour." I joined Monte for the next ten days as we made our way across Illinois, Nebraska, and Colorado. Eventually, we was going to make it all the way to the west coast.

Katie Nolan

26 Die in the Last Ditch

Perseverance, also die in harness, stick to one's text: 604a,
Roget's Thesaurus, 1947.

*By 1932 the unemployment rate had soared past 20 percent. Thousands
of banks and businesses had failed. Millions were homeless. Men (and women)
returned home from fruitless job hunts to find their dwellings padlocked and their
possessions and families turned into the street...people foraged in dumps and
garbage cans for food.*
(Nick Taylor, A Short History of the Great Depression)

Thou shalt never forget the sixth commandment, Thou shalt never give up.

1940, Bud, near Arapahoe. The last stretch between Arapahoe and the farm
hit me in the throat, then the impact travelled all the way down to my gut
and bottomed out as lead. I knew every curve and dip in the road, every
leaning fence section, every bit of scraggly pasture so well, I could feel the
landscape seeping into m' flesh and bones. The sound of the crickets beck-
oned me forward. I had chosen to walk the last six miles instead of hitching a
ride, and I was having difficulty keeping my feet churning forward, straining
with the heavy army bag that contained all my earthly belongings. There was
pleasure, pain, confusion, regret, and yes, a little anger. A flood of memories.
I struggled to get hold of myself so I could get through the greetings
of my folks.

After Harry died and I'd met up with Monte, I'd saved up on the
road. I was finally gonna be able to set down roots, most likely nearby to my
folks' homestead. I was going to risk it.

I passed Rebecca's drive, gazed up the two ruts of brown earth, smiled
at the memory of kissing her behind the barn, her curly red hair sticking

154

out against the siding, strands of it clinging to the rough boards. I promised myself that I'd go see about Rebecca as soon as I got done with the family. I'd heard that Mr. Northby was selling half his place—couldn't keep up with it anymore. Well, that would be fine, really fine. I got more and more excited as I thought about carrying out my plan. Why, I'll even make sure Mr. Northby stays put just where he wants, maybe in his old house, even if it means living on my half of the place. I wouldn't mind at all having old Mr. Northby nearby. Thousands of times on the road I'd seen myself building my own house. I'd helped Pop build a room onto the homestead so I was pretty sure I could do it. I'd imagined the foundation goin' down, the floor laid, the walls goin' up. I'm gonna set down roots!

As I strode up the dusty drive, the horizon was as bright as a newly sharpened axe picking up the morning sun. I sought out a glimpse of the porch, imagined bounding up the steps. The porch and house were still blurry against the sun's glare.

When I turned the sharp corner of the drive, I expected to see signs of harvest.

Instead, I saw the corn stalks stripped bare, and sitting dully in the sweltering heat, brown and exhausted. Furniture marched sad-like across the front yard, a hand-painted sign:

"Foreclosure."

Everything was to be auctioned off. I breathed in, quick and short breaths, and shook my head slowly, then, my head and shoulders began a'rocking back 'n forth.

I'd made it home in time to see the last of things sold, the chickens, the pigs, the iron bedsteads, all stretching ugly across the dusty yard. The cows had long since been gone, auctioned at way below the price the folks had bought them for, not worth more when there wasn't much corn to feed them. If only my folks had listened. I'd told 'em they ought to bail out, before it was too late.

I'd warned 'em with a note on a postcard sent from Chicago, when I'd stayed put awhile with Loretta. But I knew from my mother's letter that they'd hung on. My thoughts raced and jumbled as I looked on. What it looks like when everything a family's collected gets displayed in a yard.

We was left with an old jalopy and what could be latched on. So the stove was tied on, taking a few neighbor boys and Pop's shouting to get it aboard, even though Pop protested. "We can't take a stove out there, all the way West—that's crazy."

And Mom had shouted back, "We have to. How are we gonna eat if we don't have a stove." She had a point and Pop gave in. So on went the stove, a table, and a few chairs; all the food that was canned had been placed in wooden boxes and was now piled on the floor boards. Flour sacks of clothes, an old suitcase filled with family albums, scraps of lace, bits of fabric, and other useful debris of life, all were packed tight and latched shut, then tied with a rope.

In a way, there was relief on Mom's and Pop's faces. The waiting had been the worst and now it was over. They would have a new start out West. In between the relief, emotions also ran to grief and anger and hatred. They hated the bankers. They were angry at the property vultures coming for the auction. Mom cried when the first thing was sold and carted off. There went the silver tea set they had gotten at their wedding. Then, the brass bedstead. They didn't get much for 'em but they were forced to auction off what they could. I helped pack what was left.

I struggled with myself that night, tossing in my old bed so its metal springs creaked, the same mattress where I'd snatched off the wool blanket when I'd left home: Why, I can save up again if I give them what I've got. If they don't have more than the money from what they've sold, they won't have a chance. They'll go hungry. They'll never make it out West. All night in my sleeplessness, m'thinking was like a drifting morning fog.

The next morning, I shook my head slowly, sitting on the side of the bed, staring at an old top of mine that Mom had saved. It sat on a home-made shelf I had put up myself and was covered with dust so its faded stripes of red, yellow, and green were barely visible. On the road, I'd learned not to remember...not to notice. But the old toy demanded notice. With the top, the world came hurtling back, spinning towards me, dizzying-like. It was as if the top would not allow me to forget. The money to settle down would help me begin again, settle this spinning. Damn. It ain't gonna happen. I know what I have to do.

"Are you sure?" Pop had said. And I'd nodded, "Yeah, Pop. You're gonna need it." I had grinned but inside I felt heavy. There was a tug-of-war in my head. The spinning ain't gonna stop.

I slid into turmoil, but I didn't let on. As far as they could tell, I was my old self, the one who makes them laugh. I didn't have a choice. I couldn't let my family go hungry. Not when I had something I could help them with. But all of this reasoning still left my mind careening. My head was light but I felt as if my feet and legs were too heavy to carry me. *I'm gonna be on the road again.*

"You can come out West, too," I heard Pop say, over the hustle and bustle of loading the jalopy. "Might as well settle down to a steady job." But I knew that with the Depression still on, a steady job was unlikely. Pop knew, too.

"Sure Pop, soon's I get something stashed away, I'll join ya. I heard they need someone back at my old ranch in Wyomie. Gonna go out there and try my luck." I had an understanding with Pop. If he didn't push me too hard, I'd come through for family. But I could see nothing to do now but strike out on my own again. I shook my head gently as if to wake myself up.

I walked inside the house feeling strange that it was to be the last time. Mom was standing in her and Pop's bedroom with the door wide open. I stopped short 'cause I could see that Mom was frowning deeply. I'd never seen her that way and wanted to escape, but she called out when she saw me.

"Can you come here a minute?" I approached, anxiously looking at Mom. "I want you to see this. This is your Grandpa's watch. Grandpa Nolan's. I want you to have it. You was always his favorite and even though he died when you was eight, you probably remember him."

I got an image of my Grandpa, then. Of how he'd told me stories. How, not long from the old country of Ireland, the family had a memory of Irish tale-telling. And song and poetry. How my Grandpa Howard Nolan had been a boy when the Civil War broke out. How they'd fled the south because they didn't believe in the war and they didn't want their sons conscripted into the Confederate army. How Grandpa had, as a young boy, been instructed to run alongside the wagon on the way north. In that way, he'd be hidden in the brush if the wagon was stopped to conscript the boys. Then, I recalled how my Grandpa had told me of how they got started again in Nebraska, renting a small farm.

I looked up. I had barely heard Mom talking. "I want you to have it to remember him by." Mom's voice cracked a little and I looked at her hard. It scared me to see Mom suffering. She had always kept a strong sturdy hand on things and I had never seen her look so riled. She went on, "I don't know what to do with the rest of these pictures. How are we gonna have room for another box?" There was anguish in Mom's voice. "It'll comfort me to know you have the watch." As Mom had always been tough with all of us, it touched me that she shared her feelings with me now.

"Would you like to have it?" She sounds anxious. "I...I...can't lose no one."

Then, Mom forced a smile. "You'll stay in touch, won't you?"

Holding back my own feeling, I said, "Sure. Don't have no other family to stay in touch with." I tried to tease Mom to lighten things up and I took the watch from Mom's hand. I noticed the roughness of her hands, and how they shook a little as she reached towards me. I looked away and swallowed hard, working my mouth back into a grin before I looked back at her.

"Guess I'll have to leave the rest of this stuff. Can you put it in the stove for me?" Mom's voice was a bit steely, the way it got when she was angry. "No wait. Don't burn it. No. Bury it, out there," and Mom gestured to the back yard.

I nodded and watched Mom stride quickly out to the kitchen. She stuffed the one picture she had of her and Pop and all seven children into her bosom. But I could tell from her back that she was shaken in a way that she'd never been before. Her apron wasn't tied neatly and hadn't held. One side dipping lower than the other. If I'd had anybody to talk to, I would have tried to tell 'em how hard it was to see Mom that way.

I began to look through the box, unable to immediately toss what Mom had so carefully saved all these years. There was a tiny horseshoe for good luck, attached to a cardboard, and labelled with 1910, in Mom's hand.

There was a sheaf of letters and postcards from her parents, the Saylors. Then, I found the one letter I'd written home while in the Philippines. I suddenly felt bad that I hadn't written more often. There was the newspaper notice of Grandpa Nolan's death. Family history. I'd been asked to bury it.

I wanted to keep it for Mom and surprise her with it later, but then I remembered, that I can't take anything extra on the road, that I wasn't gonna be settling down anytime soon.

I bowed my head and walked out of the room towards the back yard. Mom had left for the front, where everyone was packing. This was just as well. It would be easier for her to not watch it go into the ground. I held onto it for a minute and then carefully placed it on a small mound. At the last minute I slipped the horseshoe Mom had saved into my pocket. I grabbed a shovel leaning against the back porch and dug with steady strokes. Then I placed the box into the ground and quickly filled in the hole. But I no longer felt anything. I walked out to the yard to join the others, touching the watch in my shirt pocket, feeling the horseshoe dangling in my pants pocket.

Mom was standing there, supervising it all. "Blowed out. Uprooted. Where to now?" she said. And I felt it too. Confused. "No room for anything but essentials," Mom said. "Hammers. Other tools. Gonna need tools for repairing the old jalopy. What is not essential? Keepsakes? Leave family history in the ground. Here. In the ground. Bury the box. Who knows. One of us might pass this way, dig it up. If not, we'll know where it is.

Family keepsakes. Lace. Got it from the first Nolans, come from Ireland. Heard some of 'em was horse thieves. But they weren't all bad, some had a home with those pretty lace curtains. Look at that picture, picture of Niagara Falls. Somebody went out there. All the way out there. Maybe Aunt Edie? Don't know. Who is that? Oh, second cousins. Can't even remember their names. Never saw 'em. Aunt Veda sent us a picture. Veda Lane.

She's a smart one—a writer—wrote a book, *We Live in Montana,* even put it in the library. It's like we're being blowed out twice. Not just by the wind but by some folks that don't want us here. Say they want to take this land and do something with it. Why, we did a lot with it! Couldn't have done more! Don't have no control over drought and dust storms. Where are people supposed to be? Can't be uprooted and stay uprooted forever. Need to set down roots."

We all heard Mom out and I had put my hand on her shoulder. I'd never done it before but I couldn't stop it from happening now.

"You'll set down roots, Mom, and so will I."

Mom looked startled at the angry tone of my voice. Maybe not peaceful determination but cussed stubbornness shot through with confidence. That was the kind of confidence the Nolans had.

My sister walked up slowly and frowned. "You take care, ya hear," and there was a little catch in her voice. She gave me a big hug and looked up at me with moist eyes. I was fond of Roberta because I always thought she was the one who understood me best. Why, she'd fully understood when I'd told her I'd left home 'cause I couldn't stand the yelling no more. It was Roberta who always listened with a smile, no matter what I shared. And those warm brown hazel eyes. It seems that she would approve of me even if I became a thief, or worse. This was in spite of the fact that she'd listened carefully in Sunday school to the lessons on the Ten Commandments. All of us had. For her, it seemed I could do no wrong.

"Oh, you gonna ride in the oven?" I teased her, "So's you can stay warm?"

My jokes didn't make much sense, but they always got a rise out of her and a little laugh. She hugged me again and began piling more boxes on the old jalopy. Wandah, the youngest, was easy to get a rise out of also. I'd always stood by her in church when we was kids, singing "Onward Christian Soldiers" with a twist: On a hill far away, stood an old Model T, its wheels and its hood busted in (with hood hitting the high note), and made her giggle and get in trouble. Then, I'd whisper: "Oh, you're gonna receive a knock upside your head once you get home." Then, I'd wink.

"Please go with us," they both pleaded. "We can't get on without ya. Who's gonna make us laugh? Mom and Pop need ya."

But I knew it was only partly true that I was needed, and that with one less mouth to feed they'd actually make out better. "Besides," I said, "I gotta get a job. Can't be travelling around leisure-like, on a vacation with

160

y'all—why we'd all starve if someone don't get out there and do a little work."
I grinned, then, and wiggled my ears, knowing this would cause my sisters to
fall into a giggling fit.

It felt good that I could help my Mom and Pop out, even though it
meant that I'd have to start over saving for a ranch. They didn't say
anything—their pride wouldn't let 'em—but I knew they were grateful and
would praise me to the neighbors when they said goodbye. And Mom did.

"Without Bud, my second to oldest son, I don't know what
would'a happened," Mom had said.

I thought about Rebecca, wrestling with myself. If we could work together... What if we... No. I'd have to wait until I saved up the money again. I
couldn't go see her with nothing in my pockets. Then, the nagging thought. *I
am a fugitive.*

I walked out of the old homestead's yard, only turning once and
giving a quick wave towards the back of the loaded up jalopy, then not
looking back.

27 Bird of Ill Omen

Warning, also signs of the times, handwriting on the wall: 668,
Roget's Thesaurus, 1947.

*This recession [2007-   ] is the deepest in our lifetimes, the deepest since 1929. If
you take the people thrown out of work in the 1982 recession, the 1991 recession,
the 2001 recession, not only is this bigger, this is bigger than all of those combined.*
                                                              —Austan Goolsbee

*We've been in a war and a recession. That's why accent colors with yellow and
purple are popular. They're optimistic and flirty and happy colors.*
                                                              —David Bromstad

2009, Katie, Albuquerque to Chicago to Washington D.C. Union Station
in D.C. has a fairly recently restored main waiting room, a ninety-six-foot
high "coffered ceiling gilded with eight pounds of gold leaf." (The description
is on the back of a souvenir postcard.) I sit by a fountain in the waiting room,
and admire the grandeur. This is why I travel! The time on the road is good
for reflection, then delicious forgetting. How glorious to forget all issues, listen to the fountain, and sip my coffee. But memories have a way of bubbling
up, disrupting the peace of the moment.

* * *

Right before my train trip, I had wandered about my rooms in my
cute 1914 cottage in Seattle. I felt attached to my office because I had all my
books out, a comfortable place to sit at the retro-waterfall desk, my Grandpa's homemade trunk filled with Grandma's old quilts. A runner sat on top,
stitched by hand by my great grandmother Schultz. It is a crazy quilt of velvet
scraps in a myriad of hues. Like the biblical Joseph's coat of many colors.
Good bye office.

I admired the joinery on the old chest. How did Grandpa Schultz make it? He must have had special tools and a workshop.

I went to the kitchen and sat at the fifties Formica-topped table, a gift from Audrey. I considered removing the switchplate by the door, a retro blue and yellow affair with a jolly chef and a tea kettle painted onto the plastic. No. It would just make me feel sad every time I looked at it. Besides, when would I have another kitchen where I could change out the switch plates to suit me?

The cupboards have leaded glass doors, a feature that originally helped sell me on the house. The built-in cupboards reminded me of the ones back home, and I had even been able to put my mother's set of rose-patterned dishes on display, just as she had done. A few of my mother's hand-crocheted doilies reinforced the vintage look. I had imagined growing old and comfortable right here. *Good-bye kitchen.*

When I went through the living room I felt pride in the plaster work I'd done. I'd gotten a book at the library that explained how to get a good finish and I'd ignored the advice of those around me that I ought to get a professional plasterer. I managed to plaster the holes in the ceiling myself. I went back to my office and sat down on the trunk, my head bowed to my chest, trying not to feel sad.

My head shot up. I heard footsteps pounding on the porch. My heart sped up. There had been a break-in down the street where the house had a foreclosure sign in front. Did they think I'm not home? Did my house look vacant already?

Earlier, I had turned off all the front lights to look at the fire in the fireplace. Now, it was dark throughout the house except for the faint glow of street lights. It was dead cold. The steps become furtive, exploratory. As if someone was trying to peek in the window.

I stepped carefully so as not to squeak the oak floorboards and slid out of sight, wedging myself between two bookcases. My heart was pounding. Was the bolt lock in? I couldn't remember for sure, but I usually turned it when I got ready for bed. No way to find out without being seen. I cowered in the corner of my office, waiting, listening. They tried the door. Thank god, it was locked. I heard their footsteps going across the porch, then nothing. I crouched lower, hoping my shadow was not visible. Finally, I heard them leaving down the stairs. I peeked over the window sill and saw the back of a tall man. Then, he disappeared around the corner. He was gone. I breathed. I had held my breath without realizing it.

Hands shaking, heart thumping, I checked locks on front and back doors. Why hadn't I done what I'd planned over and over if someone ever appeared to be breaking in? Simply slip out the back door and over my neighbor's fence and enlist their help. They were the kind of neighbors one hopes for, a considerate, sweet retired couple, George and Jane McDougall. Jane, who always reminds me of June Cleaver in "Father Knows Best," even brought me plates of homemade cookies! Instead of running for help, I had panicked and hidden out of sight. As if that would have protected me if someone had actually broken in!

I turned all the lights on and went to bed, reviewing my old plan of escape again and again. I decided to sleep with the lights on, and began to look at the gardening magazines on the bedside table. The glossy pictures were so very cheerful, with plans for spring flower landscapes. The garden scenes helped distract me. An hour later, I heard Eric, the downstairs tenant returning. Relieved, I drifted off, dreaming about what a large garden I am going to plant. I'd forgotten for the moment that I likely wouldn't have the backyard for planting, come spring. *Good-bye house. Foreclosure. Yep. History repeats itself, and for some reason that knowledge makes me feel better. Anyway, probably just another memory I ought to throw down some well, seal it up tight.*

* * *

Perhaps I am just tired from the long run between Albuquerque and D.C. Out of Chicago, down to Philadelphia, on to Washington D.C. I love the route names, the California Zephyr, followed up by the Silver Meteor out of Washington D.C. But I don't recall much of the landscape between Albuquerque and Chicago. Did my father have large snatches of time where he could not recall the scenery? It feels like that on the road. Like one's head is going to burst from the rapid changes in landscape.

Confessions of a Hobo's Daughter

Dear Katie,

I am now sitting regularly at Tokoji Temple. I am multiply blessed because the setting is quintessential Japan, quintessential zen temple. There is the perfect mountain, on which one may become enlightened. Please take this with humor. Then, the beautiful foot-worn stones leading up to the temple. Once at the top of the steps, one is looking down on the Strait between Kyushu and Honshu Islands, where ocean freighters lumber through, safe at last after open ocean, their cargo intact from Astoria, or perhaps Seattle, or any number of West coast ports. The temple opens onto the zen garden, you know, with the raked sand that flows around perfectly placed stones. The opening in the temple wall, long shoji screens, is so broad that one feels as if they are sitting in the garden, once on the veranda. It was on this veranda that I asked the master, again, whether it's possible to know the meaning of life. This time he wordlessly pointed above to the scudding clouds. I've spent a great deal of time trying to interpret this wordless lesson, and I've come up with the emptiness we can understand due to time. Everything will eventually dissipate, even the universe! Yet, we tend to think things like mountains or even buildings downtown Seattle are permanent. Of course, we know that they are not, at some level, it is just our tendency to think they will be there, tomorrow and tomorrow and tomorrow, ad infinitum.

So I hope this isn't too personal, but even the horrible relationships you seem to have experienced, and are perhaps? Experiencing now? Are impermanent. That is, what I'm trying to say is that suffering does not last forever. It too falls away. It seems to me that Gerald may be untrue to you. A man who never takes you to meet his friends or family, and a fellow who doesn't want you to let anyone know at your workplace that you are dating, is often a guy who is dating others on the sly.
I hope you don't take this little idea the wrong way.

Yours, Steve

PS Consider going for coffee when you return to Seattle?

Dear Steve,

WTF! You have overstepped a boundary! I asked for your opinion about my writing, not about Gerald! **And you don't know what is really going on!**

I am sure Gerald has never cheated on me!!! That is ridiculous!

The fact that he cries does bother me, but it also shows that he is not the insensitive, cheating lout you seem to be saying he is.

So, I don't want **you** *to take my little idea too personally, but you have crossed a line here. Impermanence, indeed! Cheating, indeed! I suppose there is something to impermanence, but you are so off base! I care about Gerald. He's a kind and sensitive man.*

I will never betray Gerald!

And I am not checking my email again until I return, so don't bother to make excuses for your statements. I don't need your judgements while I am trying to understand some personal issues.

Honestly!!!! K

28 Cast Sheep's Eyes Upon

Expression of affection or love, also, set one's cap, flirt: 902,
Roget's Thesaurus, 1947.

1940, Bud, near North Plains, Oregon. I approached the house where
I'd been told they needed harvesting hands. Along the drive, there was big
sunflowers, and they was tall and graceful, the way I thought tall corn looked,
and it made the entire setting look luxurious, like a gentleman farmer's.
Scattered among the sunflowers, there was some columbine and wild pansies,
holding their own, even though it was late in the season. In the distance,
rolling hills covered by firs and alders added to the feeling of life, 'specially on
a day like today when the puffy clouds cheerfully bobbed in a the bluest sky
you ever seen.

The house was a saltbox, with a long, wide front porch. Both was
unpainted, and the weathered boards looked homey.

I was filled with hope at the possibility of a steady harvesting job,
that usually includes daily meals. And the place reminded me of the Northby
place back home. I'm gonna have a place like this someday. And sometimes I
even believed it, whenever I could silence that voice that kept telling me,
"You never can settle down, you're nothing but a hobo and a goddam fugitive."

Ray, the eldest sibling at the Schultz place wanted everyone to meet me. "Oh, and my friend Bud—they call him Smiley—is how he'd said he'd introduce me."

"You got stories to tell, Bud. You've been around all right. Just wait until you meet my family," Ray had announced, again and again.

It was gonna be a late night for dinner 'cause it warn't likely to get dark until nine or so. Then, the men would come in dusty, tired and aching, but excited at the prospect of the table—Ray's sister, Nattie, got to be known for her table.

I'd arrived early and hailed Ray in the yard. I was in the habit of coming early to make time enough to smell what's cooking. Ray led the way into the house with me trailing behind him, and we both head straight for the kitchen.

"So, who's this you got with you, and you're both early!" Nattie said, wiping her floured hands on her apron.

"This is Bud, Bud Nolan," Ray said. "And this is my sis, Nattie."

"Where did ya get yer name?" I asked politely. I felt a little unnerved, the way I used to, around Rebecca. I looked at her, then looked past her head at the wall behind, avoiding her eyes, and saw that she had a wave of brown hair across her forehead that ended in a curl behind her ear. She had a moon face and sparkling hazel eyes.

"It's a Russian first name, Natalie, you know, turned into Nattie, and a German last name, Schultz. There was a time when Russia wanted homesteaders to settle the interior. So's my German ancestors homesteaded in Russia."

Now, the great-granddaughter, I learned later, carried on the tradition of farming. Every year the Schultz farm near North Plains, Oregon was swarming with activity at harvest time. First off, Nattie was now in at least her eighth year of cooking for the crew, having been made responsible for the full table since she was twelve. And a full table was expected for a harvesting crew. I imagined platters of corn from the kitchen garden, dripping with fresh-churned butter. Stacks of baking powder biscuits, to be buried under creamy gravy made from chicken drippings. Mounds of fried chicken, fresh from the coop.

168

The smell reminded me of home and I thought about Mom. She was most likely still fussing at everybody. That was her way. Now, I understood her a little better.

I noticed that Nattie looked tired, yet she was friendly-greeting all of us. I didn't know that she was also a bit worn out because she had not only been cooking for crew, but she had recently been out with Russell Graham, her fiance'. Her brother clued me in when I asked about her. The whole family, especially her three brothers, were full of winks and nods. Their little sis about to get married, and in 1940, it looked like she was almost getting too old, they said, because you were an old maid by nineteen or twenty. Still, they weren't sure they liked Russell. He was personable enough, I was told, even though as the son of a banker in nearby Forest Grove, he didn't seem to know how to do much. He was good at courting, though, you'd have to give him that. He showed up in a suit, carrying gifts. Why, he even sang in a barber shop quartet.

I gazed at the table, which was located just behind us in the dining room. I'd worked at a fair number of farms, and I'd never seen such a table! It was set with matching silverware, from the old country; the settings were Nattie's mother's wedding gift, Nattie said, when she saw me looking, and the one thing that had been brought over from Germany. The platters were blue-flowered, delicately, around the edges and bought from J.C. Penney's. Even though they were dirt-poor farmers, they sure know how to put on a spread, I was thinking. Instead, I told Nattie, "nice table."

"We might be poor, but at least we'll be clean and neat," Nattie said. It was as if she had read my mind.

I was pleased by the beauty of the setting, something I would never admit because a man ain't s'posed to care about such things. At the urging of Ray, we sat at the dining table to wait, and I could see Nattie through the wide arch between the dining room and the kitchen. I watched her as she cooked.

Slap, slap went the green-handled rolling pin across the mound of biscuit dough. Nattie probably knew, like Ma, to avoid over-working the dough so's ya get biscuits as hard as boards. I'd seen some cooks gain the reputation for making biscuits that you can use as weapons, throwing 'em like a rock.

169

A biscuit cutter is sharp-edged, its metal handle cutting into fingers a little, if gripped too hard. Looked to me like Nattie was gripping onto it like nobody's business. Perhaps it was the long nights of cooking, waiting dinner on the crews. Even when the days warn't long, she told me later, she had late nights, cleaning up, ironing her brother's work shirts, the women's dresses. Slap, slap on the dough, swish, swish of the iron—cuts and burns.

"Looks like you're gripping that thing awful hard," I said.

"Humph. It seems that everything goes sideways for me," Nattie said.

"Unless it is the up and down of kneading bread dough." I grinned at her.

I couldn't help but notice Nattie's energy, taking it out on that biscuit dough, and felt all the more attracted to her. I couldn't take my eyes off her.

"Oh, man, look at that," one of the hands exclaimed, as he entered the dining room, its long table laden with food. And it was a sight! Even more than I had imagined. The platters of chicken, corn, biscuits, the bowls of gravy and mashed potatoes, all steaming hot— and Nattie the kind of cook that waited until just the right moment and made sure her makings were served properly, hot, and on time. Then, at the end of the table, cherry pie and apple pie.

"Oh boy, oh boy!" another blurted out. All of them shouted back 'n forth—this one insulting that one about whether he even knew how to use a fork, that one asking whether he was born in a barn, all taking the banter good-naturedly. Then silence fell as over a dozen of us men set to food.

I watched her every move as Nattie presided over this, bringing more hot gravy, more mashed potatoes, right off the back of the wood cooking stove, her apron catching drips of gravy as she ladled it into the bowl. Why, she seems close to tears she's so worn out, I couldn't help but notice. Yet, it didn't look like she's gonna let on. I admired Nattie for that.

Then, the voices started up again in less than ten minutes. Five hours of labor, cleaning chickens, cooking, baking, frying and it was over in less than ten minutes of silent chowing down. I'd heard this often from Ma. Nattie said, "Why all that time a cooking and it's gone in less than ten minutes," and, "I guess you all is silent 'cause it's so good."

I was trying to concentrate on my food, but I couldn't stop watching Nattie, her curves 'specially, with the apron string tied tight around her waist, slightly sweaty, flour-covered hands, a rip in the waistband of her apron. I looked up and grinned at Nattie's comment and I thought she smiled back.

"Hey," one of the hands teased. "When you gonna marry me." He was addressing this to Nattie and she blushed.

"Go on, you," Nattie said. "I'm engaged."

I looked down at my food, feeling a big disappointment. (This was before her brothers had told me.) It hadn't come fully to mind, but when one of the other hands said it, I thought, yes, wouldn't it be nice to be married to someone like Nattie. I put that thought out of my mind right away. It warn't possible. She's engaged. B'sides, no woman will want a fugitive. I 'spose everyone who eats here wants to marry Nattie. I sure wanted to settle down. But I knew I couldn't now cause still on the run. At least I thought I had to be. What if I just ignored it? Pretended like it's over and they ain't looking for me? I could risk it. No. I can't risk it 'cause someone else would be taking the risk, too, and I can't ask no one to do that. What if I told them and they wanted... No! No one would understand the situation. It sounds like I'm a common criminal. Some folks would think I ought'ta hang. And all that goin' through my mind felt heavy in my gut, felt like yeast bread rising, pressuring my insides.

29 Sighing Like a Furnace

Expression of affection or love, also spoony: 902,
Roget's Thesaurus, 1947.

Bud, 1941, still at North Plains. Nattie often came home for the weekend.

"I heard from Ray that you're working up in the Portland Heights," I said. We were sitting at the kitchen table, where Nattie was taking a break from cooking.

"Yeah. For the Geezies." Nattie said, blushing.

"How're the Geezies?

"They're okay," Nattie said. "It's a lot better in their three-story mansion than it had been at my old place. There, the lady of the house badgered me constantly. She wouldn't let me take a rest in my room after I got morning chores done. She'd shout at the door: 'What you doing in there! Your job ain't done.'" Nattie got up and checked on her pie in the oven. Always liked that smell of warm cherry pie.

"Sounds bad," I called into the kitchen. I could see Nattie bent over the oven.

"Pretty rotten," Nattie said, as she twisted back towards me, still partially bent over. "Was nights that drove me nuts. Their daughter, Lizzie, she had some illness that stuck her in a wheelchair. All night, there'd be:

172

'Nattie Nattieeee...' and with each 'Nattie' she would get more whiny. I thought I'd go crazy as a loon."

I felt the awkward silence when Nattie paused, she maybe feeling lonely from the long speech the way I do after I go on awhile. She'd returned to the table, sat down, and looked at me uncertainly.

I thought about Loretta again, and felt the same empathy for Nattie that I'd felt for her. Nattie didn't have the scars Loretta did, but it seems that things have been tough for her. Nattie's smart, too, 'cause she'd showed me her report card from high school. Ninety words, she typed, off of shorthand.

I then remembered that Nattie was engaged and felt disappointed all over again. Why, it would be someone who was willing to work hard together, someone like Nattie, that I'd hoped I'd meet. I listened as Nattie went on. I looked at her moon face and smooth pink skin as she spoke. I could barely concentrate on what she was saying.

"Why, I vowed that some day, I'd run my own house the way I want. No one telling me the gravy is too thick and the bread too dry. I'll decide what will be cooked and how it will be prepared. But it ain't as bad at the Geezies, and," Nattie continued, "I'm going to stay a little longer, finish high school, and save up for my hope chest." At this, Nattie blushed again. I wanted to think it was because of her noticing me; she wasn't used to someone like me, looking at her face when she talked. Most guys preferred talking to listening, and I figgered Russell was that way too.

I've learned that women really like it when you listen to them. And we seemed to have a certain ease in each other's company. I wanted to try. Stop thinking about my past. Could I ask her to step out? I couldn't. Ain't fair to step into another man's ring. But Nattie deserved better, I knew that. But I decided, even so, I just couldn't. Because she deserves better than me, too. I'd leave it alone.

* * *

I was gonna go back out to the North Plains place, which alone wouldn't get my adrenaline up, but this weekend, Nattie's brother Roy was bringing Nattie home again. I had already decided from my last visit that I couldn't ask her out. I just wanted to see her.

173

Nattie had listened enraptured to my stories. Tales about travelling through Chicago, a city lit up like the biggest Christmas tree you ever saw, and stories about seeing one of the talkies, "Queen Christine," with Greta Garbo. Nattie had told me she had never gone anywhere much beyond her home in eastern Washington or, later, her home in North Plains.

I remembered Nattie saying how she had always dreamt of travel, to see the places she had read about in high school geography—Denver, Fairbanks, Chicago—even Europe. That was one of the things that gave me the idea that I might have a chance with Nattie. So, even though Nattie's engaged, maybe I can see if she'll step out with me. Why that fella she's goin' out with don't deserve her. Even though I'm a fugitive...well, it was a long time ago. I'd given up on settling down, hadn't I? All confused, I was. One moment I was feeling I could ask her and the next that I couldn't.

"Rolled into mile-high city around eight in the morning. We'd heard they was hiring at the mines, so we tried it." I was hoping I was impressing Nattie.

Monte chimes in. "Yeah, we was flat busted after them cops took us. Didn't leave us a penny. Fortunately, people in that town were generous at their back door."

I flinched and kicked Monte under the table, because I wasn't sure how Nattie would take this revelation.

Would she think me a common beggar? A tinhorn? Would she understand that you'd get yourself in scrapes and not have much choice? I gave Monte another look. Then, I changed the subject to something more glamorous.

"That's where I got the best hotel meal of my life. It was biscuits and gravy and fried chicken. I was sure I'd died and gone to heaven."

"Yeah, Bud, you always lived by your stomach." Monte was sitting back contentedly, with his fingers stuck in his waistband.

"Then, there was the Grand Opening for the Charlie Chaplin film. It was an old show but it hadn't gotten out that far west before, so's everybody was pretty excited. Charlie Chaplin himself was there, at the big Denver theatre. What was the name of that show? Oh, yeah, "City Lights." Never forget it—it told it like it is. Had us laughing..."

174

Nattie seemed enthralled. I was hoping it'd impress her because she'd told me last visit she'd heard a little about movies but had never gone—her mother believed them to be evil, from the devil himself. Movies and dances and even card playing were taboo.

I was glad her mother warn't in the room at that moment. I told about the great staircase up to the theatre proper and the chandeliers in the lobby, and none of this escaped Nattie even though she was rushing into the kitchen now and then to fetch more biscuits and gravy. She commented as she rushed about. "Well, that seems the cat's pajamas." And, "Is that right?"

For some reason, I was smitten first time I saw Nattie. The fact that she was round and energetic and laughed easily at my teasing and jokes was part of it. But there was some other quality, too, different from women I'd met so far. She was both tough and kind. She had a strong heart, I'd decided, and would be able to handle herself in most situations. She had a good heart. That was it. A good heart.

"Let's sit a spell on the porch," Nattie's brother, Lee suggested. We'd been sitting for hours, a lazy Sunday afternoon, and needed a change of scene.

As we all trailed out there, I noticed the fresh waxed floor, the bits of lace on polished mahogany, and the dance of sun through the gauzy curtains. I missed home a little, then. I wondered how they were doing after their move out west and where they'd ended up.

I was goin' to look them up first chance I got. I hadn't lit any one place long enough lately, for them to send me a card—I guessed I'd better let 'em know where I was. My emotions churned a little, but I didn't let on. I was good at grabbing hold of myself, distracting myself, moving on and leaving the feeling behind.

"You've been around, Bud. You ever think of settling?" Nattie's brother, Ray, said.

I blushed a little, and so did Nattie, because we both happened to glance each other's way at just that moment.

"Sure. I reckon I might."

Nattie quickly looked away. I wished I knew what she was thinking.

I had been coming to the Schultz farm every weekend for a month. I'd pitched in to work on the farm every time, even when they didn't have the money to hire hands, so they were glad to have me, and began treating me like family. This night I was feeling that just maybe she'd talk to me, maybe even go somewhere with me. No! I couldn't ask. There was the fiancé. But I didn't take him very seriously, the couple times I saw Nattie go for a ride in his car. For one thing, he seemed like he was vain, showing up in that suit, and waiting in the parlor. He's the kind of guy that would complain about maybe there gonna be a flash flood when you tried to picnic on a river. I had never seen him lift a finger around the place—what kind of man wouldn't help out? I didn't understand what Nattie saw in old Russell Graham. A dandy, in my book.

"I've gotta go shut in the chickens," Nattie said to no one in particular. She paused a moment.

"Need some help?" I saw my chance to talk to her alone. I was barely aware of what I was gonna do.

Nattie stuttered a little at that. Her sister, Maxine, and brothers, Lee and Roy, exchanged knowing glances.

"Well, uh..." Nattie said.

"Oh, you two, go check on the chickens," Lee chimed in. He had never liked Russell and had been pretty noisy about it. Maybe he wants Nattie to go out with me, a sure way to break it off with Russell. Saved by her brother, Nattie nodded and off me and Nattie went, down the side of the house and to the back, where the chicken coop stood about twenty yards from the saltbox.

I spilled out: "I've been wondering...that is...I've been wanting..." I took a shallow breath, "Would you go to the County Fair? You know it's coming up next weekend and there's gonna be all kinds of excitement, some things you might like." My heart pumped awful fast-like.

Nattie said, "That'd be swell." Then our hands brushed as we both reached for the weathered wooden latch to shut the chickens in for the night, to protect them from the coyotes.

My week flew by at the sawmill. All I could think about was Nattie's face, how she'd looked in the moonlight next to the chicken coop, how she'd smiled and looked so pleased when I'd asked her to go to the fair. Then, I'd go on thinking about how it felt when our hands brushed. Before I knew it, I was heading back to North Plains.

It had been arranged. I would pick her up for the County Fair the next morning, Saturday at nine.

Later, Nattie's mother shared, "Even though I didn't like Russell that much, I sort of felt sorry for him. He just sat under the old apple tree and cried."

Me and Nattie had managed not to let slip the fact that I had been a hobo—we thought it might worry Nat's mother, even though I was ready to settle down. And I had never mentioned that I was a fugitive to either one of them. I wasn't intending to take that chance. Not yet.

Courage is a funny thing. You might muster the courage for one thing and not another. I'd had the courage to choose Nattie. For now, I could not overcome my other fear, that of being abandoned, or worse, if'n Nattie found out my secret.

And some parts of what had happened, well, I wouldn't even allow myself to think about it. That pushing a memory away tires you out sometimes, though. Always pushing it down and here it comes, surfacing. Gotta will it *not* to have happened.

30 Flying Fish

Unconformity, queer fish, half-caste, half-blood, half-breed,
cross breed, mulatto: 83,
Roget's Thesaurus, 1947.

*Miscegenation, coined ca. 1863, marriage or sexual relations between a man and
a woman of different races, esp. in the U.S. between a white and a black,*
—Webster's New World Dictionary, second College Ed., 1984

2009, Katie, on the train near Jesup, Georgia. Is that where it happened?
I wonder, as I travel through Georgia. Sun-dappled dirt roads wander off
through the oaks, draped with kudzu vines, vines clinging to life, and in
their aggression strangling the life from the trees. Is that where he ran? Is that
where he feared for his life? Is that where his terrible secret manifested?

I try to imagine my father as a young man but all I can conjure up is
one picture of him standing by his 1940 Ford. A picture that had sat on my
mother's dresser. I have it now, and it graces my bookshelves at home. In the
picture, he had his trademark grin, and, according to my mother, he still had
a dramatic shock of thick dark hair. My mother had often mentioned what
great hair he had when she met him.

I am distracted by a young woman settling in the seat beside me, her
long legs kicking at her satchel to push it under the seat. She has to duck to
avoid hitting her head on the overhead. She'd gotten on at a quick stop in a
little town. Even though I had tried to see the name of the place, I hadn't

Confessions of a Hobo's Daughter

been able to catch it on the rail station. All I knew was I'd recently passed through Jesup.

She tells me she is from Jamaica. We sit quietly together for quite a while, after the first greetings, where are you from, where are you headed, how long have you been travelling, what's your name, that sort of thing. Her name is Jill.

Then, I notice that Jill is gazing down at my laptop perched on the seat tray. "I'm trying to write a love scene," I explain. "And it is difficult."

"Oh, I love romance novels."

Ah, I think, an expert. I don't tell her that what I'm writing is not a romance novel.

So I ask her "What makes a good love scene? What are you looking for?"

"I want to know what's in the minds of the lovers. What they are thinking and feeling." Jill reads my three-page love scene and it elicits a tepid response. "Oh, that's interesting."

I begin to apologize for its deficits. "Well, it's difficult because it's between my parents. I had to give them different names and pretend it wasn't them to be able to write it."

Jill laughs. "That is a challenge!"

"Yeah, one I'm not sure I'm able to carry out. But I have to know that my parents were young once—and they loved each other—that's kinda nice since I was a product."

Jill nods but then becomes silent as she looks through her fashion magazine. Something I have rarely done and I suppose it is obvious from my lackluster wardrobe. I wonder if I were to look through such magazines whether the ideas would rub off, in the way that looking at decorating magazines has earned me the reputation of being able to put together a room. In fact, I have done such a good job of decorating with furniture from Goodwill that friends have recommended that I freelance as a budget decorator. I try trading magazines with Jill for awhile but I can't get interested in fashion.

We both put down the magazines when Jill begins speaking. "You know, on a long trip like this and reading your piece makes you think. I've been thinking about my boyfriend back in Jamaica. I came here partly to get away."

"Really, I'm travelling partly to get away, too. But the things I am trying to escape, seem to have come along for the ride."

Jill smiles. "It does seem to work that way, doesn't it."

"Well, I am travelling to write, really."

"Where's your boyfriend from," Jill asks.

"My boyfriend is from Nigeria."

Jill raises an eyebrow. I think uh-oh. This is what Gerald always says. Some black women will hate you because they feel like white women are taking their men. I didn't want Jill to hate me.

I wait. With relief I hear her say, "Well, that's brave of you. Not everyone can handle it. Lots of pressure. Sometimes even danger. I heard they call it miscegenation in the U.S. Why do they call it anything?"

"Good question. I think it's a political issue. To keep people separate. I read where the powers that be were threatened by poor whites marrying black men, especially early on with the indentured servants getting together with enslaved Africans. Thought that they might revolt together, so they made a law against miscegenation."

"And you still have the problem..." Jill's voice trails off.

"Well, yeah, I think Gerald and I couldn't comfortably take a road trip across the U.S. Maybe have to avoid Idaho! Well, probably parts of the south, at least some places."

"It's a strange country..." her voice trails off again.

"How long have you been here?"

"About two years." She pauses. "So, do you love him?"

I begin to stutter "...umh...oh...I..."

"Where's all that doubt coming from?"

"Well, our lovemaking...then..." I blush.

And Jill rescues me with her rejoinder. "Men are such clods!"

"Well, what do you mean?"

"My man, back in Jamaica is a hunk—but he ain't no kisser, man. I try to teach him..."

We both start to laugh. Relaxed by the chardonnay, second glass, and the rhythm of the train, I share my problem with kissing.

"Well, he's a good-looking guy, too. So I want to kiss him. I try to tell him to be gentle, not so hard. But he pushes hard and practically breaks my neck, and the tongue! He won't kiss me gently, just the pressure and the tongue and enough pushing to knock me over if I don't hold my ground. I am suffocating and barely able to stand up! But occasionally, when he does kiss me soft, it makes the bottoms of my feet tingle."

"That ain't love," she says. That's possession." I can't respond. I hadn't thought of this before. Possession. "And you got self-esteem issues, girl!"

I can't respond to the latter, either. I just move on, shifting topics. "I have doubted whether he loves me. For one thing, when we break up, and I admit that it has been mostly me doing the breaking up, but him, too, he always tries to begin things again by calling me for a date. No comments come from him on our recent break-up. Well, it seems that neither of us want to talk about it. About what happened. You'd think I would have figured this all out by now. I mean, I was lucky in that I had a role model from my parents."

"That sounds pretty typical. Guys don't like to talk about the relationship. But, hey, that's pretty lucky that you had a role model from your parents." Jill nods encouragingly.

"They really did love each other. I heard them often, giggling into the night. And when they were younger he used to pick her up when he came home from work and carry her through the house."

I smile at the memory of my parents. At the same moment I'm beginning to feel agitated. Possession? Self-esteem issues? How can Jill know these things?

I recall how, when I'd been flattened emotionally, not certain I could get up off the floor and move on, I had said to myself: "Well, fake it until you can make it!" That became my mantra. What is this? Is she right?

"So what are your real names?" Jill brings me back.

"Oh, my parents are Bud and Norma O'Shea, and my name is Susan." When the names roll off my tongue, I feel confused. I had begun to think of my father as Bud Nolan! And my mother as Nattie. Natalie Schultz. And myself as Kate. Katie. Kathleen. I really like that name. Then, I realize how powerful names are. Katie Nolan is really a different person from Susan O'Shea. And, what if I'd been named Agnes?

181

Interestingly, my father told me once that the people on the road only used first names. That's why, even when he got to know someone pretty well, just a first name is all they had. Loretta. Harry. And any number of other people. Caleb. Benjamin. Silas. Simon. If you pressed for a last name, someone might think you're a cop. (These still aren't actual names, including O'Shea. Out of habit, I gave false names to Jill. Maybe I still do need to keep this under wraps, is what I was thinking. Who knows how it would affect me for people to actually know the truth about my family's past. Or my past, for that matter. Or, what I think.)

"Well, I'll look for your book."

"Thanks. But I did want to ask you another question. Do you think a big secret between lovers keeps them apart?"

"What kind of secret?"

"Say they are a fugitive from the law, or, say they have a crazy family member living in the attic. Shouldn't they tell the person closest to them? Their lover? Especially if it is a committed long-term relationship."

"Of course that would keep them apart. If they aren't sharing everything important, they are eventually gonna separate."

"You're probably right." I take a deep breath and sigh. I think I knew what Jill would say but I feel rather stupid for asking such an obvious question. "Thanks for the conversation. We are almost in Savannah. Is that your stop or are you going beyond to Charlotte?"

Jill is getting off in Savannah. I decide to do the same, but I don't try to meet up.

31 Bestow One's Hand Upon

Marriage, also nuptial tie, knot, one bone and one flesh, be spliced: 903,
Roget's Thesaurus, 1947.

Bud, 1941, still in North Plains. I sat with Nattie in the parlor, and we
leaned into each other on the small couch. We were both looking out the
window at the low clouds and the early morning mist.

Nattie sighed, "It's beautiful."

I looked down at her and grinned my widest grin, "Yep, pretty fit to
be seen."

We were newlyweds and the drizzling rain of North Plains, Oregon
seemed beautiful, even uplifting. And that's the way Nattie was. Even if
something warn't so purty, she'd say, "Well, that don't look so bad."

I walked up the steep stairs to Nattie's room and carried down the
suitcases. We were almost on our way. Nattie slid into the seat beside me,
the vinyl of my old jalopy still smooth and neatly stitched, only worn on the
driver's side, where the edges were a little frayed.

Nattie glanced back at the house where she'd tearfully said goodbye
to her mother and sister and brothers, even her brother Roy, that had always
whipped her. Now that she was leaving, she'd forgiven him.

The car bounced down the lane, almost bottoming out on its axle at a few of the ruts. Nattie was saying "Don't ya think you ought to slow down? Or this old buggy ain't gonna make it." She said this cheerfully and teasingly, but there was a hint of worry in her voice. I'd already noticed that about her, her seeming to worry about most everything. I sped up a little, looking over at her and grinning. "Oh, you," Nattie said, and she laughed a little.

"Oh my gosh!" I said, with as much alarm as I could muster so that Nattie really began to worry.

"What? What's wrong?" Nattie bit.

"I forgot my wallet."

"Oh, no," Nattie groaned.

She was quiet all the way to the end of the drive. She was probably thinking about how we would be delayed by at least two hours. One hour to return for my wallet, where I'd been staying near the sawmill, and a second hour to backtrack.

I looked over at Nattie's worried brow. Done teasing her, I pulled it out from my back pocket, "Naw, it's here."

All Nattie could do was splutter, "Oh, you big tease. Don't you do that." But then we both laughed.

Even in the drizzle, I felt a sunny warmth. We had shared dreams, our shared hopes of having a place of our own. Nattie said it had to have a rosebush in the yard, a picket fence, a few chickens, and be a big, big ranch.

At the end of the drive, we turned down a firmer gravel road, that eventually shifted to pavement, then onward toward the Oregon coast. As we chugged along, I tried to think of a way to tell Nattie she'd just married a fugitive. But should I? Would she understand? I chewed on it, worried it, half the trip to the coast. I just can't tell her. Should I tell her? Finally, I brushed it aside. I'll deal with it later.

We arrived in time for a late lunch and enjoyed a plate of the best seafood we'd ever had.

"Oh, you can't eat all that," I nipped off a piece of her cornbread, seeing if I'd get a rise out of her.

"I can too!"

"What do you want to do after lunch?" I asked her.

"Let's go down on the beach. I remember they rent bicycles built for two down there and I always wanted to try it." Nattie had seen couples on the bikes when we'd visited the one time before we'd been here and she had dreamt of doing that, she explained.

"Sure, honey. I can peddle ya all the way to Chinee."

"I'm sure you can." We were getting to know each other, and we likely both held too many painful secrets to make it easy. I still had the urge to tell Nattie about my past, my being a fugitive. I wanted to tell her.

"You know, I ain't told you everything 'bout the road."

"We've got lots of time for that," Nattie breezily said.

"Well, it got pretty rough sometimes. A guy had to fight to survive." I took a deep breath.

"I heard that some men even got to be criminals, but I'm glad you ain't no criminal like the others." Nattie looked up at me, smiling. The moment was gone, then, when I might have told her. Because shortly we'd arrived, and a man was before us saying, "twenty-five cents an hour." I felt relieved. I guess I won't tell her on the honeymoon. But those words were with me: *I am a fugitive.* I knew I'd need to tell her sometime.

Twenty-five cents seems like a fortune, but we didn't care. The day was unusually warm for the Oregon coast, with a gentle breeze and a hot beating sun. Nattie hadn't had much experience on a bike but I had and I liked showing her the ropes. That is one of the things that I admire about you, Nattie said, how you take charge in any situation and make things work. You have a charmed life, Nattie added. I was thinking, she don't know the half of it.

"Do you think we can get all the way to that rock down there?" I was pointing to an outcropping that rose hazily just offshore but far down the beach.

"Sure we can." And off we went, one of our first destinations since the wedding. On the way back we found a photographer on the beach who offered to take our picture. It was a great shot, me peddling in front, and Nattie in the back, in her shirtwaist dress, store bought she'd said proudly, hugging her ankles, and skimming the anklets folded neatly above her new oxfords.

It was our good fortune to find one of Long Beach's finest, a beach cabin with a quarter moon cut into the shutters. Inside, it smelled of salt and sea. We turned on the electric heater and set about to make some coffee and pull out the cookies we had brought along. When we sat down and realized where we were, we just looked at each other, happy-like and fed each other bits of cookies, left on the plates at the end of our snack.

I recalled what makes a woman happy. I kissed her on sweet spots I'd learned beforehand, courting her, then, began to undress her slowly. Made sure my fingers brushed down her neck gently, then across her breasts, stroking them through the soft linen of her travelling suit. Nattie sighed with each touch, so I was grateful I was pleasing her. She said it was a revelation—what it felt like for a man to touch her all over. I unbuttoned the linen top. Her hat had long since slid off the chair as we brushed past it. The skirt slid to the floor. I lifted her up and carried her across the floor, making her laugh, giddy-like. We slept cozy and warm.

I stopped thinking about my past. I was able to completely erase my memory of it, for the moment. In fact, I didn't even think again, about what I was gonna have to tell her, not for the entire honeymoon.

32 Fiddle-faddle, Flapdoodle

Absence of meaning, also twaddle, twattle, rubbish, rot: 517,
Roget's Thesaurus, 1947.

2009, Katie, Georgia, then New York. This train is loaded on its east coast run going north, so I am uncomfortable. Usually, I can stretch out luxuriously on two seats, the advantage of being short, but every seat is taken, including the one beside me. Orlando, Jacksonville, Savannah, all these cities are unfamiliar. We had no relatives this far east so we never had travelled this area on our camping forays.

Savannah, where I had gotten off the train to be alone, to think about things. I spent two days there, wandering around among the oaks graced with Spanish moss, enjoying the architecture, not getting any closer to figuring out all the connections, so I could really answer the question, What's at stake?

I spent hours online and at the Live Oak public library to no avail. They kept some records for the chain gangs, but I couldn't find anything about my father. There was an interesting list of people jailed, and one of the names may have been Dad's brother, Bob. His father's name was on the same list, Clarence Grover Nolan. Surely, that must have been Granddad, as how many Clarence Grover's can there be? To be sure, his rum running might have gotten Granddad time. And Uncle Bob was definitely on the road also. But the research was disappointing. I wanted to find out whether Dad was right to think that the guard had died. Maybe the guard hadn't died.

Perhaps the lack of familiarity in the south is also disorienting, and doesn't help me to focus. Self-esteem issues? Possession, not love? Those comments from the woman from Jamaica really got to me. And I am still seething from that email from Steve. My god! What drivel! Well, like Jill said, all men are blind to what's going on.

Jill got me thinking. I suppose my sister and mother both not wanting me around could have contributed to self-esteem issues. I wouldn't blame them, of course, but these little things that happen sometimes do affect us. My sister always found me "ugly" and would complain to my mother about what I was wearing. "Don't let her go looking like that!" my sister would exclaim. My mother had me convinced I was "bad." I suppose this would help explain my desire to disappear constantly.

Actually, it is beyond desire—after I've been going for a bit, seeing friends, working with my writing group, I feel compelled to disappear. I mean, like anxious compulsion, the way one feels when someone is after them. I have to get away and be by myself. But I've taken care of all that, haven't I? I grew up. I gained confidence and I got degrees. It all just makes me feel confused. Maybe I'll have a better handle on it later.

It is a gloomy night, the air in the train is stifling, and I am having strange dreams about my boyfriend, Gerald.

We are together, running from the government police (he had told me stories about his work for independence in Nigeria). We hide inside a cement dam, surrounded strangely by cotton, recently picked and unmilled, and lying side by side one another, as if we are corpses. Then, he goes over the falls, me despairing and trying to save him.

I wake to the snores of my seatmate. I've gone down on my knees and laid my head on my crossed arms on the seat bottom. And I am chilled from the cool draft blowing along the floor. My back feels like a truck has run over it, and my head is pounding. Talk about wanting to get away! I want to be anywhere but where I am, contorted and wracked with pain, on this swaying train.

I am on my way to New York. There I will have a brief stopover to see my friend Martin Moreau, who'd recently left Seattle to try the east coast. We'd been through graduate school together, and after years of thinking this young man was just being kind to the older returning student, I began to realize that he actually liked talking to me. Well, I'm not completely sure. But I am fond of Martin.

He meets me at the station and we go to a charming fifties New York diner. I order apple pie and Martin has a corned beef on rye. We settle into the booth, aiming to catch up. Martin's hair is coarse and black, sprinkled with just a tiny bit of salt, and contrasts with the orange booth behind him. His dress is stylish bib overalls, that make him look cute. I am thinking that it ought to be easy for him to find plenty of dates, yet he often complains about how hard it is to meet someone.

I begin the conversation: "Do you still think love is all a delusion, a made-up thing? A social construct by those nasty western Europeans?" I say the latter jokingly. Martin is from France, and many of our conversations have been centered on our love lives, our love problems. Well, being from France may have nothing to do with it, but there it is, the French as experts on love. In any case, I always learn something when we share our respective dilemmas.

"Well, yes. Don't you?"

"I don't know."

"Oh come on, we've gone over this many times. Love doesn't exist. It is just another bit of the social construction of reality. Romantic love was an invention. Designed to keep us in line. Designed to make all of us into good little consumers. Move into the suburbs. Have several kids. Buy an SUV. Buy furniture. Romantic love, or the idea of it, has caused so many problems for people." Martin pauses.

"Do you ever feel love?" I ask this rather urgently. "I mean my love life stinks. I have not felt like, oh, what a wonderful time I'm having, ever."

"Oh, that's terrible. Why?" Martin asks with sincere sympathy.

"I don't know why. But back to my question. Do you ever feel love?"

"Well, yes. I feel it after every girl passes me on the street."

We both laugh. Well, so much for romantic love in the hands of two philosophers. We had finished our doctorates in philosophy at approximately the same time. Our heads were filled with anti-essentialism, nothing has an essence. Postmodernism. Plato, with his ideal Forms, was wrong. There is no ideal Form for love. Certainly, romantic love has no essence.

It doesn't technically exist, because something has to have an essence to exist. If it has no essence, it simply isn't. And who knows what makes love what it is? "Love simply does not exist," Martin assures me.

A year later, when I heard from Martin and was invited to his engagement party, I somehow felt betrayed.

* * *

I go to a zendo in New York, one recommended by Audrey, my friend I'd met long ago when I'd lived at the Tibetan monastery in Seattle, and, eventually the woman who had become my best friend. She was a most irreverent type of Buddhist, taking the newly arrived monks from Tibet to the movie, "Rocky Horror Picture Show." She'd been asked to show them around. She told me that they laughed heartily and enjoyed it very much. I think she took that concept, that the sacred and the mundane are the same thing, rather literally! It still makes me smile when I think about it.

Before we settle onto the zafus, the Roshi gives a zen talk. "There are four thoughts about phenomena that assist us to turn our minds toward a meditative life, toward enlightenment. Phenomena is temporary. Phenomena is not innate. Phenomena is impure. Phenomena does not bring happiness."

I have intellectually accepted this many times. Yet I remain caught in a web of desire for romantic love. No matter how many times I remind myself of the fourth thought: *Phenomena does not bring happiness.* The reason a love story is so seductive is that it *does* bring short-term happiness. A true love story brings heaven on earth, I'm told. Really, I wouldn't mind having that experience! But, alas...

Perhaps I am closer to some clarity. Heaven on earth is nothing compared to the self- possession and peace that comes, close to enlightenment. Yet, even an enlightened woman lives on the relative level where she practices her ethics and learns to love. The web of confusion loosens ever so slightly. Perhaps it is necessary to work on my psychological problems, to work on myself, before I can get to egolessness, or *no-self.* I still desire to live my love story but it is becoming a more aware desire. Perhaps I need to live my love story, to get closer to an enlightened self. Would living an aware love story have its place on the path to enlightenment? I'm excited about this new possibility, this new insight.

I almost consider sharing the insight in an email to Steve, then remember how he's trampled on what I'd shared in writing class. So I can't understand why I am even checking for another email from him. Argh! He owes me an apology. Nope. Not a thing from him online. Shit! What am I looking for? More punishment from him? More impertinence! I can't understand why my heart is racing as I glance through my inbox. Why am I even thinking about Steve?

* * *

Back on the train, leaving from New York and heading for Toronto, I recall another conversation I'd had with Martin. I'd told him that Gerald had woken up at three in the morning and, when I'd discovered that both of us lay awake, I took up the earlier fight we had had that evening. It had been a six hour fight! About housework. I had insisted that when a man and a woman live together they share the housework. Fifty-fifty. No exceptions. I reminded Gerald that I was a feminist and not just any ole feminist, a radical one. And he had insisted that that wasn't important. That one just hired a maid. I had been outraged. A maid! No. That is classist. One cleans up one's own messes. It is just exploitation. You ought to know that—you who claim to be a socialist! And we went on and around, arguing over what it means to live together, about housework, about you name it...

Martin had looked at me, astounded. "You don't fight about housework at three in the morning. That's when you should be making love."

I then felt bad about what I'd done. I supposed Martin was right. Ignore differences. Let love happen. But I couldn't.

"We are so different," I'd told Martin. "I don't think it is just about housework. I grew up on a farm. He has no interest at all in that lifestyle. Not even in how it was for me, growing up."

"It sounds to me like you might be a little afraid of intimacy," Martin had said gently.

"But Martin, that is definitely not true. And you always told me to avoid that psycho-babble, you know, not psychologize all our problems, if I was going to be a good Marxist."

"That's not what I said! Being a Marxist doesn't mean you don't have psychological problems. That just wasn't what I said. And I'm not even sure we ought to be Marxists. You don't seem to understand the problem of psy-chologizing."

"But all our problems are not up there in our head! You know, your-self, what I am talking about. I hate all that new age stuff when it diverts people from really noticing what the system is doing. And it leaves out com-pletely an anti-capitalist analysis."

"Katie, your problem is that you are mixing analyses. It's okay to separate them, you know."

"Martin, it really is not me that is afraid of intimacy. It is him, Gerald!"

"Well, who knows, maybe both of you."

I hadn't been satisfied with Martin's last response, but I'd decided to let it go. I'd changed the subject.

"Well, I am trying to see how my father's story contributes to all my confusion about relationships. There is a lot there. I know my father's tales influence my politics. You know, it has to do with perception. Growing up knowing that the police and the system are not on your side does color your world. Knowing your father was friends with a Wobbly organizer is different from if you were, say, the son of a mayor or a congressman. Or, the daughter of a businessman."

"How is the writing going?"

"I am getting down all the scenes that my father told me. It is more difficult to see how these stories have gotten in the way of my intimate life."

"It seems obvious to me." Martin can always be counted on for an opinion.

"How is that?"

"Your parents, particularly your father, taught you to be a fighter. To survive. That's the opposite of teaching you to be a lover."

192

"Oh, Martin, I wish it were that simple. Then, I could just stop fighting..." I'd taken a deep breath and changed the subject again. (I did have a fleeting thought as to whether this might fly with Mickey. *I am a fighter not a lover.* I made a note in my journal.)

I'd told Martin about our little dairy when I was growing up that eventually didn't make it when dairies, like other farming, went corporate. He'd glanced at me sideways but let me off the hook.

The memory of this conversation with Martin about my parents and the farm reminded me how much I had enjoyed doing farm chores with my father. He whistled his way through them and was always joking. I enjoyed the smell of the cows, pushing my head and shoulders into their flank to make reaching their teats easier. Their udder was warm. We milked into smooth stainless steel pails, teats, udders, buckets, hands, all carefully scrubbed before we began. I smile into the dark face of the train window, remembering doing the chores with my Dad

Part Three

Extract Sunbeams from Cucumbers

33 With Head Erect

Pride, also dignity, self-respect, not think small beer of oneself: 878, Roget's Thesaurus, 1947.

1959, Bud, Green Mountain. Hunched over on a three-legged stool, I worked an udder, then drew down on a cow's teat. I liked the sound of the swish into the bucket. I got Katie to giggle when I squirted milk toward the cats. The cows were contentedly munching hay, having determined their own order of things, each choosing her own stanchion and sticking with it. They'd come up the trail in a single file, walking with ease, gliding each into place in the big pole barn.

Gene, my sister Roberta's husband, had helped me build the barn over a period of two years. I had begun by first cutting the trees for the poles off the back forty, then fleshing out the pole construction with siding. I'd cut the cedar shakes for the roof on weekends, all by hand. The barn now rises its two stories with pride. Some fellers have come along and photographed it. Painted red and surrounded by green pasture, they say it looks like a Norman Rockwell painting.

"You want some?" I said.

"No." Katie smiled. And I aimed at Katie, like I had the cats, as she laughed and dodged and danced near the barn door. A four-paned window near the door let in a ray of light that filtered down on the straw scattered across the floor.

"Hey, come on over here and learn to milk. See, here. Push the edge of your hand up in there. Now put that first finger and your thumb right there. Hold your finger and thumb in there tight and squeeze from the top down," I told Katie. "And look out for the hooves. They're likely to stick a hoof in the bucket or kick it over." I looked on while Katie concentrated on the matter at hand. There were twenty-four cows to milk, so everyone needed to help.

I watched as Katie struggled with the full stainless steel bucket, trying to lift it up to pour it into the ten gallon milk cans, Route 984 painted in crude red letters across its neck. Katie had learnt to raise it partly with one of the fronts of her thighs, making it possible to maneuver more weight.

I looked up at the spires of rafters, the sharp peak down the middle of the barn, wondering to myself how I'd built it. But I did! I patted my grandfather's watch in my pocket and thought how proud Mom would be.

If only I could've gotten rid of the dark cloud that seemed to sneak up on me when I started feeling content. A cloud that involved the secret. I'd hoped I could share it with Nattie. Shouldn't she know what's goin' on if they ever come to get me? But somehow I knew that it was likely too late to tell Nattie now.

34 The American Dream

American dream, the U.S. Ideal according to which equality of opportunity permits any American to aspire to high attainment and material success: Webster's
—New World Dictionary, second College Ed., 1984

2009, Katie, north of New York City. Perhaps that is one of the Great Lakes! I am on my way to Toronto, Ontario. I note the wisps of fog along the side of the tracks, drifting up from the water. My life in a fog, the saying echoes in my head. I rummage through the minutiae of my relationship to Gerald.

Don't forget how he brought soup to me every day when I had the flu. And remember how he drove me to work, even though it was quite a ways out of his way. Think of all the times we went out to early dinners at Anthony's and enjoyed the sunset! It's too easy to just recall the problems!

I had glanced up from my reveries on the positive, when I recalled our work life together. It seems that much of the time spent together had been in his office, him holding court.

* * *

Many others flow through his office and it often feels I am waiting my turn. When I stand in the hallway, I can see past Gerald in his office chair, to the campus lawn beyond that leads up to a classically covered ivy wall.

199

Seattle University, even though it is in the midst of downtown, has these beautiful lawns, old stone walls, and intimate courtyards.

Gerald's office is spartan, few books lining the walls. On the shelf above his desk, he has a large glass container filled with chocolate. Even though the snicker bars inside are my favorite, it is several years before I get up the nerve to ask him for one.

Once inside his office, I sit more prim and proper than is my usual slouching self, a habit I got into growing up rural, where it was somewhat acceptable. I hadn't thought about it before, how much of my natural self gets occluded when I am with Gerald, knowing intuitively that he would be critical. He jokes sometimes about me being a hippie, but I know that he doesn't really approve of the way I dress. He always praises me when I reluctantly put on a power suit. You know, a Hillary Clinton kind of get-up. In my case, an ill-fitting suit jacket from Goodwill.

My mind wanders, my mother saying to me, when I told her I was about to get my doctorate: "You'd better not be gettin' on no high horse. I hope you'll still be able to mop a floor."

Gerald breaks into my train of thought. "People will think that it is a Horatio Alger story. You know, the American dream."

Maybe, if I told him what my father really went through, he'd understand better. But I just can't tell him that my father killed the guard to escape. I don't know why I can't tell him, I just can't. Instead, I jump in with my argument: "Oh, no! It is not the American dream.

There is no such thing. For oppressed groups of people it is the American nightmare. You know, the indigenous people that died in geno-cidal proportions, the history of slavery followed by segregation and all that oppression afterwards. The working poor who get minimum wage, or immi-grants who get less than that." I am really getting worked up. "In most cities, you can't even pay your rent and eat on minimum wage, and you certainly won't have health insurance!" I rush through the list, speaking staccato-like, and spilling anxiety into the room.

"Well, I know that, but that is what people are going to think about your story."

I am deflated. I leave his office trying to figure out how to change the story so people will see the nonsense in the statement "You can achieve whatever you want to, if you want to badly enough." But how can I get that across? Our fate is in our own hands in one way, but it comes about that it is often intertwined with the fate and greed of others. Of course that doesn't mean that we shouldn't try our level best to achieve our dreams. Work against whatever befalls us. My father showed me that.

The next time I see Gerald I repeat all these things to him, having carefully rehearsed them in my mind, first. He stubbornly refuses to accept the logic. He repeats: "It will be read as an American dream story."

I want to shout at him. "What do you know? You who think we should have maids? Why can't you see the problem with that!" But I don't. I just make excuses when he asks me to go to dinner, knowing that he wants to spend the night with me. I know I won't be able to have sex while I am so angry. Instead, I wave gaily at him as I pass by his office window. He has no idea I am upset.

I go home and distract myself with my class prep. This lesson is one of my favorites, really, all about Descartes and doubt. The poor fellow doubted whether he existed or not. And I really relate to that. I always enjoy presenting the punchline to students: "Cogito, ergo sum," or, "I think, therefore I am." I follow my preparation with a hot bath and wrapping myself in my favorite soft robe. Then, I thumb through the latest Better Homes & Gardens, amusing myself with garden plans. I feel a little triumphant that I didn't succumb to the temptation of agreeing to an evening out. That is something I have done in the past, trying to please whoever asks me, not really knowing how I feel.

Perhaps I would be jolted out of my numbness if a man came along who understood how important it is for me to feel the earth with my hands. Well, Gerald would never understand. So why don't I leave him for good? We really could be no more different from one another. Class difference. Race difference. Gender difference. Even sexuality! One time I had risked telling him I thought everyone was bisexual. That I'd gone out with a woman once and maybe... He didn't respond to my comment.

* * *

I lean my cheek against the glass, after pushing the small curtain out of the way. Night has fallen and indistinguishable city lights flit by, making me wonder where we have gotten to. The coolness feels good, because for some reason my cheeks are hot, as if I had just experienced my most embarrassing moment. The rolling along of the train seems to help. The train doesn't stop, even when I am feeling static and blocked from movement, my body frozen stiff in the seat, my cheeks still burning.

35 Much Cry and Little Wool

Disappointment, also slip 'twixt cup and lip, non-fulfilment of one's hopes,
one's countenance fallen: 509,
Roget's Thesaurus, 1947.

1961, Bud, Green Mountain. "You'd better bathe if we're goin' to town.
Don't wanna go looking like some yahoo." Nattie was repeating this for the
umpteenth time.

"Oh, what do I need of it." I grinned at Nattie, teasing her, because I
knew she'd win out.

"What do you need of it? For goodness sake, you're gonna stink if
you don't."

"Stink. Nobody's gonna notice."

"And put on those clean clothes I laid out."

"Clean. You're gonna wear 'em out washing 'em so often." Nattie
sighed and shook her head.

And this went back n' forth, as usual, all the while I was getting
undressed for a bath in our built-on bathroom that barely fitted in a sink and

a bathtub. But Nattie was thrilled to have indoor plumbing. Nattie turned on the water and drifted back into the kitchen, fussing with things for supper.

Our 1940s Ford bumped along the gravelled Lewis County road. Me and Nattie were on our way. The nearest town was forty-five miles. And as was Nattie's habit when I fell silent, she said: "Penny for your thoughts."

"Oh, nothing."

"Nothin! How can you be thinking about nothing?" Nattie said. "Your problem is that you don't trust no one to tell them what you're thinking. Well, someday, you're gonna have a problem if you don't. If you don't get some things off your chest, it eats at ya."

I knew Nattie was right. But now it's impossible to tell Nattie about the chain gang. How could she understand what I did? And what if she judged it? How could I burden her with it? Besides, she had once said that I warn't a criminal like the other hobos. I preferred that she continued to think that way. I decided, for the moment, What she don't know won't hurt her. I began to tease her.

"Got any money?" I said, grinning my best grin.

"Why, no. I thought you had some."

"Oh, faloney," I said—I often did this to tease—combined two words. In this case, fiddle-faddle and baloney. And I could see that Nattie had started up worrying that the purpose of our trip wouldn't come off.

"You don't..." Nattie began. And before she got any further, I pulled out my wallet and a few hundred fell out.

"Oh, you..." Nattie said, predictably.

"There for awhile, looked like ya got the wrong sow by the ear." I looked at her crosswise.

"I'll teach you how to grab a sow," she said, grabbing my free arm hard and shaking it.

Nattie came back strong, but she couldn't hold onto the anger in her voice, 'cause I had gotten her to laugh.

I looked over at Nattie and grinned at her again. Nattie smiled back, shook her head, and rolled her eyes.

Early next morning, I shifted over to my side of the bed. I had just made love to Nattie, and although I always enjoyed it, occasionally I felt confused afterwards, a mental cloud taking over. I avoided disturbing the blankets, slipped my body out by staying flat against the bottom sheet and sliding, then heaving both legs over the side without sitting up.

I wanted no response from Nattie. Perhaps it was mornings like this that I was carrying out my vow to pretty much watch yourself, better not get too attached, 'cause you're likely to get abandoned down the road.

I headed quickly for the coat closet in the kitchen, grabbing my old brown coat, black-stained from oil on the sleeves. Once down the steps of the back porch, the mental cloud began to lift, the smell of fresh cut cedar kindling, strong in the woodshed. I whistled the tune to Mockingbird Trill. Then, I reached the barn door, again felt the pride in having built it myself, admired its long posts and cathedral roof. I concentrated on filling the buckets. I headed back to the house wondering if I'd have to reduce the herd again, after the bad year for hay. Inside, Nattie was busy in the kitchen, preparing breakfast.

"Hungry?" Nattie asks. She kept her back to me.

"Yep, hungry as a starved coyote."

Nattie served up the pancakes, eggs, bacon, oatmeal and coffee without saying anything else.

36 Put the Saddle on the Wrong Horse

Error, also labour under an error, take the wrong sow by the ear, reckon without one's host, take the shadow for the substance: 495, Roget's Thesaurus, 1947.

1961, Bud, Green Mountain. Nattie was riled but I sure didn't know what about. All she'd mentioned was that I'd slipped out of bed awful fast yesterday morning. All I'd done is rush outta bed to go milk the cows. Whenever she got irritated, I headed out to the back forty. I looked up just in time to see a small herd of elk on the hill above the barn, and just next to the fence line separating the pasture from the forest. Good sign. Should be able to get an elk and put plenty of meat in the freezer. That ought'ta please her.

I entered the house via the woodshed, then up the steps to the back porch, a long extended affair with a workbench all along one side, then up a second set of steps, where Nattie had her Maytag and laundry trays. When I stepped into the kitchen I could smell the cornbread. It mingled with the smell of ripening pears in two wooden boxes, set just outside the kitchen door.

My boots, filled with dirt I'd tracked from the spring and the swamp along the creek, started dropping mud across the kitchen floor. I grabbed the broom and began sweeping it all into the dustpan, while I watched Nattie's back as she worked at the stove. She had on a red polka dot apron she made herself, out of a worn out dress. When Nattie heard me, she turned around and saw me with the broom. "Whatcha doin'?" Nattie said, both puzzled because I don't usually sweep, and maybe pleased because I'd come back. "Oh, nothing," I responded, grinning. I walked over and hugged Nattie from behind as she continued to stir the pot. "What's that you got cooking?" I asked.

"Oh, you can see, can't cha?" There was a little edge in her voice but Nattie began to smile in spite of herself. I tugged at Nattie's apron strings so her apron slid part way off. "Oh, you, stop that! Get out of here!" And Nattie laughed and threw her apron at me.

37 Slip 'Twixt Cup and Lip

Error, also put the saddle on the wrong horse: 495,
Roget's Thesaurus, 1947.

2009, Katie, Toronto to Vancouver B.C. I am crossing Canada on the Canadian version of Amtrak. There are acres upon acres of rock formations and scrub between Toronto and Vancouver B.C. The gray stone, often eight or more feet across, overlaps one over the other, so that it lays low and flat, like small, lengthy waves across the land. It is sometimes referred to as the Canadian Shield and the pink and gray rocks date billions of years ago to Precambrian time. I am fascinated by it as there are no people living on this land, which is impossible to farm. Then, suddenly, after miles and miles, and where there is enough topsoil, one comes upon little farming communities.

I wistfully think about how, in the past, one could homestead in Canada. They wanted people to settle this vast area of its center. I long for a little farm of my own as I see the neat farm houses and outbuildings. I recall how much my father loved his farm, even though it was not exactly the big ranch he had dreamt of. He was waiting to retire from logging so he could finally get to that back twenty acres to clear more ground.

I sometimes wonder whether things are not working out with Gerald because he simply does not live up to my father's standards. I mean, Martin is just wrong that it is me that has the problem with intimacy. It's much more complicated!

Gerald is the furthest thing one can imagine from a farmer. I suspect Gerald secretly judges people who work with their hands as inferior. Of course, he would never admit this. I can't imagine Gerald and my father in the same room together, and somehow it feels as if my father would not approve of him. I'm sure he would have never voiced his disapproval but I would have sensed it from my father's body language and expression. For one thing, Gerald has never worked with his hands. Also, he drinks when we go out, something that continually disturbs me. My father could fix anything. And my father was not a drinker. In fact, he refused the invitations to stop off at the bar with the other loggers.

Dad wanted to be with his family and to be part of the evening ritual. Every night we sat at our places, me, the youngest, sitting between my mother and father, my sister to the right of Mom, and my brother to the left of Dad. The round oak table sat close enough to the wood stove to warm us. Dad kept us all smiling or giggling with his teasing, sometimes outright rib tickling for the youngest. Then, "Look, something is in your ear," he'd say to my sister, Theresa. "You can get it out by wiggling your ear—here, like this." Then, he'd wiggle first one ear then the other. Quite a feat!

When Theresa giggled, her hair she had done up on pink foam curlers bobbled up and down. She patted them back into place. She was the daughter who cared about how she looked, going to great pains to be up with the latest styles. Someone else has said that families assign roles to each child and it is difficult to change this later. My sister's role was "the pretty one." Even her name, Theresa, was pretty. She avoided doing barn chores and spent lots of time in the bathroom. My brother was the smart one. He was going to go to college and rise above being a farmer or a logger. He eventually got a scholarship to MIT. And me, I was the tomboy. I seldom set my hair, unless my sister nagged me to do it, and my long straight tresses were a bit mousy, according to my sister. I preferred outdoor chores to the kitchen. I loved sitting on the ground beside Dad, handing him tools, when he worked underneath the car.

The table was laden with at least five things every night. Sometimes more. Mom worked hard at this, canning every free box of apples that came her way, putting up a root cellar's worth of fruit and vegetables from her expansive garden. When things got out of hand after harvest in the fall, Dad would sometimes help with the canning.

The entire family helped with the haying, including uncles, aunts and cousins. I walked barefoot across a stubble field to take a large pitcher of iced lemonade to the crew, only flinching when my bare feet happened upon a Canadian thistle. With any luck I'd get a ride back to the house and barn on a large pile of loose hay on the hay wagon.

My father didn't express his appreciation for the well-laid table overtly, but he demonstrated it by lingering over every dish. "Corned beef hash" made from leftover roast beef, corn on the cob, home-canned pears, warm baking powder biscuits, and fresh-from-the- oven wild huckleberry cobbler, the latter a special treat on his birthday. "Mmmm...what's this?" he would say, as he picked each dish up and placed a big helping on his plate.

Nattie might say, "Guess you liked it because you practically inhaled it." And he would nod with a wide squinty grin. Meals were generally a happy occasion, and the only sin you could commit at them was to not clean your plate. Well, other sins were possible, such as the one I committed one particular night.

I had just been pushed down by my sister so I sat down at the table struggling to not cry, a bruise on my left elbow smarting where I'd gone down hard on the linoleum. It wasn't working. I couldn't choke the food down and my body shook with silent choked-back sobs. My mother noticed first, and with disgust in her voice stated emphatically, "Straighten up and eat your dinner!" My father frowned his silent disapproval which made me try all the harder to stop the sobs.

I don't recall whether I managed to eat my plate of food. All I remember is choking on it and trying so very hard not to cry. Thinking about it still feels uncomfortable. And it has been over fifty years ago! My mother tried to silence me by telling me how ugly I was when I cried. "Your face is going to freeze in that ugly expression if you're not careful," she'd said.

The train is still rolling through Canada and for that I am grateful. It helps me put this memory off to the side, to leave it on a side track, as if it is an unhooked boxcar. I feel silly that I can still feel the pain of the childhood moment, the anxiety of choking back the tears.

That's it! I finally think I know what's at stake! Women need to express themselves! Not repress. Cry when you are sad. Smile when you are happy. Say how you feel and speak up with what you want. Not, "Wouldn't a picnic be nice," but "I want to go on a picnic." Not, "I've heard that finger-tipping is delicious, where your lover drifts their fingers over your entire body," but, "I want to try finger-tipping." I've got to learn to say directly what I want. To express myself! If only I knew what I wanted in relationship to Gerald. I can't even imagine him doing such a thing as finger-tipping. He's the kind of guy that if asked for a back rub, he brushes his hand across your back, awkwardly, once or twice!

38 Silent as a Stone

Phrase meaning taciturnity, also, silent as a post, hold one's jaw, mute: 585, Roget's Thesaurus, 1947.

Thou shalt never forget the third commandment, Thou shalt never grieve.

2009, Katie, still rolling through Canada. Of course we all die. But my father thought he'd not make it much past his youth. Yet, he lived to see the Cowlitz River dam go in. He lived to see the volcanic explosion of Mt. St. Helens and his farm covered with inches of ash. He lived to see the flourishing of life after the layer of ash washed away.

He endured, like the Cowlitz, a river that was in some ways lonely, carving away at the rock of the foothills of the Cascades. The river continued until it achieved its path, sometimes tumbling in narrow passageways and sometimes relaxing in deep pools where the rock gave way to make a wide channel.

It was in these deep pools that I swam with my cousins. No one taught me to swim. I learned by watching an older cousin, scissoring his legs and moving one arm over his head.

The side stroke. To this day, the side stroke is the only way I can swim. It made such an indelible impression on me it is as if I am stuck forever with this stroke.

The river has not chosen its path alone. The rock could only fall away in its time. The making of the canyon depended upon the rock. The river had to wait upon it. It cannot choose its source, a spring high in the Cascades. It does not choose its path down the mountainside. The people of this landscape have had to push forward like the river, bound by the force of gravity to go toward the ocean, limited in their freedom by twisting and turning around obstacles, until both have left behind only traces of their existence.

* * *

In 1993, an ambulance carrying my father wove past vehicles on the narrow winding road that led to the Cowlitz River bridge. It sped across the Cowlitz span on its way to the Chehalis hospital. Chehalis was not rushed, even at five in the evening, with slant sun on the 1920s buildings, causing a rosy glow on the pink brick. Main Street was quiet, a few farmers' pickups rolling slowly toward old Highway 99 to return home with their heavy bags from the Albers feed store. Farmers' wives picked up staples from Albertson's, a smaller version of the city supermarket, and poised on the edge of town, where old-fashioned lawns with picket fences left off and pastures, surrounded by barbed wire fences or cedar rail enclosures, began.

The hospital on the hill just above Main Street sat silent, as if holding its breath, while inside my father lay still. His fringe of gray hair, slightly too long around his ears so it looked ruffled, was pressed against the flat pillow of his hospital bed. If he had been able to choose, he would have stayed home. "Ohh...we can't afford it," he would have said, and managed a grin in spite of the pain.

But he had not been able to speak, and my mother panicked and called the ambulance when she saw him collapsed by the woodshed, with bloodied fingers, which he had swiped across his face and down his shirt, so it had looked like a terrible bloodbath. So one can't really blame my mother for her panic.

Now, I stood by my father's bed and noticed his shortened fingers laid against the crisp hospital sheet. My father's third finger on his left hand, and part of his fourth, were inches shorter, having been pulled into the blades of his power saw when the whizzing chain caught the edge of his glove when he passed out and fell. A barely visible spot of blood contrasted with the white gauze, wrapped around and around each finger, emphasizing the stubs, then crisscrossed atop his hands.

I looked over at my mother, curled in fetal position on the short couch which was shoved against the wall beyond the foot of the bed. The institutional orange plastic couch, with stainless steel arms at each end, barely fit her torso. Her weeping, only back and shoulders heaving and no sound, tore at me, reached my heart. But, instead of being able to console her, with a word or gesture, I watched her as she lay alone in her grief. I am ashamed of the memory, but I observed her the way I did as a child, still not sure of what she might do or say. Why can't I say something to her?

My mother wore her turquoise polyester pantsuit, one she had made herself, and I noticed that the pant legs were pulled up, the way pajamas pull up in the tossing and turning of difficult sleep. I remembered that this is why my mother always said she'd never wear pajamas. Instead, she always wore a silky short nightgown. Does Dad feel sad when he thinks he might never brush up against that silky smoothness again?

My father turned his head away from me. He had a vacant stare when I tried to engage him.

I whispered, "Dad, they never caught up to you." Hoping for a glimmer of a smile. Nothing. I was still the only one in the family who knew his secret. And now he might die, we'd been told by the doctor.

Of course, I'd kept my vow to not tell his secret to a soul until after he was gone. But I couldn't even think about my father dying. I held on to hope. Maybe he'll pull through. Against the odds. Like he always had.

Earlier, all the grandkids had stood round his bed, some with tears in their eyes. "How are you, Grandpa? We love you, Grandpa." They had taken turns. They left the room, looking sadly at each other. My brother touched Dad's shoulder, then quickly looked away. My brother was the one who had called me to come. When I had asked him, How bad is it? he had responded with, "It is hard to see Daddy this way." I knew then that I had to come right away. My sister approached the bed tentatively, smiling and saying, "Hello, Dad." Then, they both left. I had barely felt my siblings' presence in the room or their trailing after one another out the door. I sat vigil.

My father grimaced. One leg jumped under the loose white sheet. I knew he would not groan. If he had ever felt any pain during his life with us, and I'm sure he had, he never let on. I felt that the only way he would be able to release some of the pain through a moan, was if I left the room too, but I sat frozen in place.

My father looked at me, and even mustered a grin. My long straight hair was irritating me by falling into my face and I tossed it back over my shoulders. I fidgeted, flashed a grin back, while I uncomfortably slumped in the hospital chair. It was shaped like an old-fashioned barber's chair, with a bend in it at just the wrong place for someone short, causing the top of my torso to be shoved forward at an awkward angle.

I was anxiously preventing myself from crying, which took the form of frequent swallowing and shoving my tongue against my front teeth. I wanted to please Dad, who I believed wouldn't approve of such a display of emotion, even now. My father half-closed his eyes in a slight frown. I sat frozen awhile longer, at a loss as to what to do. I finally got up and patted his foot. I tried rubbing it, thinking it would distract him from the pain. He frowned more deeply and shook his head no. Feeling helpless, I replaced the sheet, then pulled the curtain around the bed. I slid away from the curtain. I felt an anxious desire to stay, but I didn't want to disturb Dad.

I walked slowly to the door, glancing back at the curtain. On my way out, I tried to distract myself by using my finger to trace the nicks in the Formica of the small counter next to the sink by the door. I leaned against the counter for a moment, trying to breathe.

It was the third day at the hospital and no one had slept.

My mother had left the room, now me, and my brother and sister had gone home earlier. I sat outside the hospital room on a little plastic upholstered bench, its uncomfortable cold penetrating through my jeans. I felt pressure under my eyes, then stinging, then two thin lines of tears dribbled down my cheeks. I stared at the gray wall just feet away in the narrow corridor.

I looked up and saw my mother approaching with the usual sway in her walk. I quickly brushed away the tears. April Morris, the nurse, and a family friend, came down the hall behind Mom. She said hello and asked Mom how she was doing.

Mom said she had to go home, so I agreed to drive. April looked at us tentatively then said, "You know with that heart, this might be the night..." her voice trailed off.

Dad died during the night. I have never forgiven myself for leaving him alone. I had heard April but had pushed it aside. This still haunts me, and whenever I begin to feel the least bit content, my gut clinches with regret. Then, I tell myself that sometimes it is hard for people to die when people who love them most are clinging to them, unwilling to let them go. To handle the regret of leaving him there alone, I have to believe that my father knew he was going to die and wanted, needed, to be alone. I still do.

39 Extract Sunbeams from Cucumbers

Impossibility, also make bricks without straw, milk a he-goat
into a sieve, weave a rope of sand: 471,
Roget's Thesaurus, 1947.

The tenth Nolan commandment, Thou shalt be authentic.

2009, Katie, still rolling through Canada. I stuff my journal and pen in
my backpack and wander through the train. Multiple tourists snap pictures
from all directions in the lounge car. We are travelling through the Canadian
Rockies. I know I should feel excited. While I do enjoy the scenery, I don't
have the energy to enthuse about the craggy peaks.

"So close you feel you can touch them." That's what it says in the
train brochure. I grab my throw-away camera and join the others. It helps
to have the distraction, the excited voices around me. I feel somewhat lonely
watching the happy tourists. The loneliness is difficult to admit.

Dinner reservations are called, so I make my way there, a little un-
steady from the combination of the wine I'd sipped for the last couple hours
and writing the hospital scene, along with the train rumbling and swaying. A
couple sits opposite me in the dining car. They explain how they are taking
time off from the University of Ontario, where they teach, to take this trip.
I notice in a flash a loving glance from the husband, as he looks down at his
wife. It is as if a quick shot of warm energy is exchanged between them. I
could swear I saw tears of joy in their eyes.

I felt it then. My stubbornness. That cussed stubbornness of the Nolans. My numbness. The strangeness of not being able to cry. Yet, even now I want to defend *not crying* as a good trait.

*So it is **me** that has a problem with intimacy! Martin was right. And Steve was right to point out to me the obvious about Gerald. Tears sprang to my eyes, when I realized I'd blown it with Steve. What an idiotic email I'd sent! If only I could take it back! No wonder I feel so disjointed, so isolated. I've blown so many moments when I could have been close to people. Here I am smiling at that couple across from me, all the while these emotions are rising.*

I feel relief when dinner is finished. It takes so much energy to fake it! I walk, dazed, back to my seat and grab my journal. I suppose the real question is not why I saw how my numbness affects intimacy after a thirty-day writing trip across the U.S. and Canada, but why I didn't get it years ago. Mom and Dad, I accept that the fault is mine to own, but may I hold you partly to blame? Not personally but just by virtue of our joined fate? It was the two of you who set the standard. Big girls don't cry. And all those commandments! So that is how I judged myself (and others)!

My problems with Gerald, and all my other lovers, are neither due to class differences nor my inability to tell my lovers what I want. In fact, my failure at love has not been caused by anything on my list, including alcoholism. Mickey is right. It goes much deeper and it is more about the survival messages my parents instilled in me via the Nolan commandments:

Thou shalt turn the earth.

Thou shalt keep it close to the chest.

Thou shalt never grieve.

Thou shalt always appear calm.

Thou shalt be a good judge of character.

218

Thou shalt never give up.

Thou shalt keep steady one's roots.

Thou shalt not put on airs.

Thou shalt get on with it.

Thou shalt be authentic.

My god, we were a stoic lot! They wouldn't have had an answer if I'd asked Mom and Dad: "How on earth can I be authentic if I have to be careful about who I trust and what I share? And if I must never cry?"

At the first chance I get, I call Mickey.

"I've learnt it's *me* that has a problem with intimacy while I've always thought to blame it on the emotionally distant guys I was with. I guess it has taken a few conversations with friends and going through these family memories to figure that out. Along with noticing that every time one of those family stories was told, the Nolan commandments were reinforced."

"Well, that is quite an aha moment. You've known all along what's at stake...the reasons for your inability to have a loving relationship... I just wanted you to explore it more deeply..."

I paused to take this in, then spoke hesitantly. "Thanks for never letting me off the hook. I think." Then I harrumphed, my usual nervous, ironic laugh. "I was frustrated as hell sometimes by those repeated questions of yours. It caused me to writhe in fetal position on the floor sometimes. But at least I found out what I needed to know. So I guess that's good."

"Don't stop now. You have just a bit more exploring to do. You know. Childhood trauma?" My heart descended to my gut, which was riled like a panicky goldfish, flopped out of its bowl onto the floor. More exploring? More childhood trauma? Do I really want to dredge up these memories? I already felt turned inside out.

"Okay," I say, forced effervescence in my voice. "But I am so much closer. I'll call again when I get back." I realize she is right, but it doesn't make it any easier.

"Okay, sweetie. Talk to you then."

It feels like the phone hangs itself up. My stomach is still flopping, my head is reeling, my temples are throbbing, and it is impossible for me to focus. *She knew all along? Damn.*

40 Bait with a Silver Hook

Motive, also, the why and the wherefore, gild the pill, what's at stake: 615, Roget's Thesaurus, 1947.

Thou shalt never forget the third commandment, Thou shalt never grieve.

Thou shalt never forget the second commandment, Thou shalt keep it close to the chest.

2009, Katie, Seattle, then Cowlitz River bridge. I get off the train and bump my wheeled suitcase over the cobblestones at the Seattle station. I wonder if anyone will be there to meet me. Then, I realize I'd not told anyone when I was arriving. Better. I can't stand emotional greetings. Or worse, what if I mention my time of arrival and no one shows up? Then, I catch myself. That is how I used to be. It is just going to take time to digest the insights I've gained. I am anxious to get to my car and head to the Cowlitz River bridge and Green Mountain.

I want to visit my parents' gravesite before I settle back into Seattle. It is four in the morning when I pass through Salkum, a small berg near the bridge. In the stillness of the early morning, I stop beside the sign, "No Stops on the Bridge." A three-quarter moon shimmers on the lake below. For a moment, I see the beauty of the landscape, what the deep gorge once was, with moss and ferns clinging to the rocky sides, the spray of rushing water keeping them moist, and now what it has become, a lake that fills up the gorge and spreads over the more shallow sides, to nestle against the firs and alders, the moon lapping intimately toward the trees. Then, a shadow occludes the image, the way a dark cloud battered by the wind creates a moving blot on the ground.

* * *

I was eight years old and I was afraid of heights. I willed myself to not look over the edge of the Cowlitz River bridge. I had to look. My stomach went queasy when I peered over, three hundred feet down the steep, rocky sides of the canyon. The world spun. I shut my eyes. That didn't work. I opened my eyes a little, squinted until the world was flickering like an old movie reel. I swayed back and forth, then dropped down and felt the hard pavement on my bare knees. I gripped hard on the lower railing, shoved my head between it and the railing above.

"God damn! Katie," my mother said, "Get away from that edge!" I pulled myself up, stumbled back a step, watched my mother open the trunk. Then, my mother came round the side of the car holding a squirming gunny-sack close to her side.

"God damn," my mother muttered to herself, "impossible to feed them," as she struggled towards the slightly elevated walkway along the guard rails, the gunnysack writhing.

I watched her from a few feet away, dragging the gunnysack along the pavement. I watched her struggle to get it to the top of the railing, part of its weight pushed up with her thigh. I stared at the heavy oxfords, wondering if she would trip on the long, loose lace.

The top of the gunnysack was tied with baling twine. The life in the sack had shifted so part of the moving and wriggling bottom of the sack, nine puppies, now hung over the edge of the top rail. I wanted to cry out but I knew better because that shoe would come off easily since it was already untied. My lips trembled. My mother gave me a hard look, and said a bit breathlessly, because she was still holding onto the heavy bag: "Don't. You. Dare. Cry." I bit down hard until I tasted blood. My mother shoved the sack over the rail and it began its slow descent.

A gust of canyon wind picked up a corner of the sack and sent it sideways. It landed hard on the rock ledge next to the river. The sound of whimpering puppies rose up from the canyon. I heard my mother's voice, distant, strained, choked, almost a whisper, "God damn..."

I wanted to scream, "Please...No," but I held my breath instead. I gripped the rail and shut my eyes tight. Tried to imagine how to climb down to the ledge.

"Get in the car," my mother said. A hand jerked me up from the pavement, shoved me toward the car door. I reached up for the handle and pulled at its dull silver with both hands, feeling like my chest would explode. I climbed up onto the seat, swallowed hard, set my jaw, and bit my lip again. My mother was already waiting in the car. I sat rigid and upright in the passenger seat, tasting the warm trickle of blood. The car sped off, the railing a blur when I turned my head to look out the window.

Back home, I heard Dad say, "Well, did you get rid of the puppies?"

"Yes, but you're gonna do it next time. It was pretty awful." Mom said.

"Not much else we could do. No one wanted 'em and we can't afford a vet." Dad's voice trailed off so I could barely hear him.

"I know. But I'm still not ever doing that again." Mom's voice was emphatic.

In the morning breeze, I still hear the whimpering puppies. I think about how they had no choice. How long ago the river patiently rose with the snow melt from deep in the gorge, and took the unwanted puppies into its current. If the puppies had not been taken by the river, they would have starved or been devoured by a coyote.

It was in this landscape that that first Nolan commandment, *Thou shalt never grieve*, was first brought home to me. I learned to expect loss in life and to never let on how I felt about it, no matter how much knife-like pain coursed through my body. A version of the commandment, "you can't trust no one, *keep it close to the chest*," was introduced long before my father shared his terrible secret with me. In my child's eyes I felt, *I can't trust anyone, not even my father*.

Heart still racing, I leave that now widened span due to the dam, noticing the low guard rails that have replaced the arches in my rear-view mirror. I head my car toward Swofford Valley cemetery.

Once there I squat on the ground next to my parents' shared stone. The sunrise warm on my back, the earth beneath me alternating shadows and light from the scudding clouds, I begin to weep.

I wept because I had not understood my mother's pain. Did my mother have a choice? If I had understood Mom, maybe I could have helped her. Maybe I could have comforted her when she was visibly distraught that the puppies had missed the water, the gunnysack taken up by the wind currents. Maybe I could have saved the puppies.

I wept because I loved my mother.

I wept because my father, courageous in life in every way except the one he really needed, died without sharing his secret with his wife. He neither gave nor received the trust and love he deserved.

I did not weep like Vivien Leigh in "Gone with the Wind," crumpling gracefully to the ground, the way I'd always imagined I would. I wept like me, ugly and tear-stained, hair sticking to my teeth as the wind whipped it into my mouth.

I wept due to the secret that kept me from sharing freely, first with my mother, then, with my husbands and lovers, keeping a distance between us that neither I nor they understood. I wept because of the isolation that comes with keeping a secret.

I wept because I followed the Nolan Commandments, which had never allowed me to weep, or to trust enough to risk love. I wept for all raised poor people who live by similar commandments.

In the end, I wailed, doubled over and flattened like a midnight candle, rocking on my heels beside my parents' grave.

Dear Katie,

Please accept my apology. It was totally out of line to comment on your current boyfriend. And you are right, I don't know the context. I did it without a terrible motive, even though you may not believe this now. It is the case that I wanted to ask you out for coffee. But that is not why I said what I said. I just got carried away with my ideas about impermanence, etc, etc...
S

Dear Katie,

Please, please forgive me. I was way out of line, commenting on Gerald the way I did. I promise not to do that again.
Yours,
S

PS I still want to go to coffee. How about it?

Okay. Okay. I wasn't going to check my email. But I can't help it. And every time another email comes in from Steve, my heart pounds. What is that all about? I mean, it is not like he has asked me out or something. It is just coffee... It is awfully sweet that he hasn't given up, even though I've ignored his emails for a couple of weeks, now. And he hasn't even commented negatively on my rude email. In any case, I owe him an email, and an apology.

Dear Steve,

I guess what you said about Gerald hit too close to home. So, I do realize that you have been partly right, especially considering what I had shared with you. For example, each time Gerald seemed so out of line, there was an explanation. Even the time Gerald ate in front of me and didn't offer me dinner. Do you remember when I told you about that? I think it was after writing class one night.

To be fair to Gerald, I had recently told him that I was vegetarian. Then, that night when he ate dinner without offering me some, just offered me ice cream, I had told Gerald a few days before that all I'd been eating lately for dinner was ice cream. Sometimes seeming mistreatment really is just mis-communication.

It's taken my new knowledge gained from reflecting on my family past, and on Gerald, to see my part in all this. I think we may never be absolutely finished with reflections, explorations. Each effort seems to bring new insights.

But this has been brought home to me! It really does take two to tango!

Best,
K

Should I send that email? I didn't really apologize. And maybe it is too revealing about how unfair I've been to Gerald. Then, before I could think about it further, I hit send. How many times do we do that? Hit send, then, it is too late to take it back! Well, now I've really blown it with Steve.

And wow! How could I forget Gerald's side of things! It makes me ask whether the same is true regarding my first two husbands. This insight has gotten me rambling in circles, in this little wifi cafe on Highway 12, saying to myself, Oh my god. Oh my god. Oh. My. God. Until I notice the waiter looking alarmed at my muttering. For his sake, I abruptly sit down and write in my journal.

Jerry, my second husband, was depressed and tried to share with me, one time, what that was like. He often used the phrase "black dog of depression." It is embarrassing to recall now, but I had no understanding of depression and did not give him the empathetic audience he deserved. No wonder sex was a problem for us. Sex is playful and fun and that is just not something one can achieve during a deep depression! Maybe I could have helped him!

Wayne? We married too young! He was only twenty years old when we tied the knot, certainly not ready to settle down. He must have been overwhelmed by the responsibility when that first baby came along. Then, when I recall how

226

he submerged himself in television every weekend, how he wasn't up for doing anything, I wonder if he was also depressed? He likely was. I was too self-involved to even try to understand. Maybe if I had understood we could have worked things out.

*It is **me** that has a problem with intimacy.*

41 Played Out

Phrase meaning epilogue, also, set at rest, once for all: 67,
Roget's Thesaurus, 1947.

To begin with, the same qualities that go to make a fulfilling relationship—qualities such as love, commitment, forgiveness, surrender, and honesty—are also the qualities that contribute to our spiritual growth.
"...the nature of our spiritual lives is reflected very much in the quality of relationships we have. In this way they become an accurate mirror."

—From *Chop Wood, Carry Water: A Guide to Finding Spiritual Fulfillment in Everyday Life*, eds. New Age Journal, p. 36, Jeremy Tarcher, Inc.,
Los Angles, 1984.

2010, Katie, Paradise Bay, Olympic Peninsula

"So were you guys starting things up again when Gerald came out to see you?" My best friend, Audrey Blanchard, is so direct, something I really love about her. As mentioned, we'd met years ago when we lived across the hall from each other in the Tibetan monastery in Seattle. It was a boon for me that we both had found retirement homes on the Olympic Peninsula, Audrey in her RV on a little plot of ground, and me on ten acres and in a tiny 8x16 camp trailer, sitting on what I call Forest Farm.

"Oh, no! It was good you were there when we came by," I'm saying. "Because I didn't know what to do with him. I mean, he is certainly not going to help me with my vegetable garden. Or with building a cabin."

"It seems ideal. He doesn't demand much. Not around much. Isn't that what you wanted, so you could write?"

"No. I want someone who is out here helping me with my garden and building. A person I can trust. Someone who loves the earth, like I do."

"But you said you didn't want someone around a lot. That you need lots of time alone to write. That's what you said about that fellow you met in writing class, what's his name?"

"Oh, yes, Steve Anderson. He's wonderful. But I may have blown it with him. He said something personal in an email, I took it the wrong way and lambasted him. Now, I'm a bit embarrassed."

"Well, you seem to be caught in those famous contradictions philosophers like to talk about. But I notice you seem to light up when I say Steve's name." Audrey has that smile she gets when she's teasing.

I laugh. "That's really confused, isn't it. Okay. I don't know for sure what I want. But I know I'm not so numb now. I think I could even trust someone and love them, so even though it's scary, it is also exhilarating. And what a relief to have finally made a decision about Gerald. And to decide not to return to my old life in Seattle."

"You were numb?"

"I guess I have been."

"It sounds to me like you were never madly in love with Gerald."

"Probably not. But it is hard to tell since I've been numb for so long, not driven that way since I was eighteen." I use the shorthand reference to explain my numbness but I know it has more to do with all those Nolan commandments. Do all raised poor people have trust issues? Doubt themselves? Doubt everyone? I suspect so. This is just all too new to me to try to explain it to Audrey.

"Right!" Audrey says. We both laugh.

"But it is all a delusion," Audrey the Buddhist says. "Right." I agree with her.

"But it is a fascinating one." Audrey flashes her gorgeous smile.

"I've wondered why write a novel when it is only and always about delusions." I say this with excess earnestness.

"I love novels!" Audrey says. "Sure it's a delusion but it's real people's stories!"

"And they are that, stories that we make up, not real." I emphasize the not real. "

"True, but some things seem to be real, like suffering, like poverty, like war, like love. And I've learned that meditation alone doesn't work, if you don't also resolve your psychological problems. Novels sometimes help people do that."

Of course I agree with Audrey on this.

"It's complicated," I say. I look at Audrey and smile. I vow to myself once again to stop following the Nolan commandments.

I plan a meditation retreat, at Audrey's urging. She loans me a Buddhist book, *Golden Letters,* which explains Dzochen-style meditation, something she's recommended.

Then, goodbye Nolan commandments! (Maybe I'll keep a couple of them, like, *Thou shalt turn the earth*, and, *Thou shalt never give up.*)

The tears come (they seem to come quickly these days) and Audrey doesn't seem to mind. She puts her arm across my shoulders and we walk along the sandy beach of Paradise Bay, in silence for awhile.

I break the silence. "Maybe I'll take dancing lessons. On the train, I met this nice couple from Lincoln, Nebraska that were in their seventies and did square dancing. That inspired me."

"Square dance lessons?" Audrey says, and laughs. "I can see you doing that. You can twirl in your skirt and look like that dancing zen master you told me about."

"I told you about him?"

"Oh, yes. I loved the story. Of course you might want to switch and make love to a different type of teacher. There isn't much future in an affair with a zen monk." We both giggle. "And you ought to respond to Steve's email. Just go to coffee with him."

"I *am* going to meet him. We have a plan for next week, to meet at Saddle Up Espresso. From there, we are going down to the beach for a picnic." I smile, recalling my first meeting with Steve. His lanky frame leaning against the door jamb to the classroom at Hugo House. Those green eyes! How I was impressed with his writing on zen and the art of living-off-the-grid. I *was* attracted. And it was sweet that he apologized in those emails, even though he really hadn't done anything that terrible.

Staring down at my tennis shoes, rising and falling against the sand, leaving their distinctive patterned footprint, I show Audrey a dance step I'd recently studied in a book on tango. "Leave it to you, to try to learn to dance from a book." Audrey says. She tries it too and we embrace in a tango down the beach. We collapse on the sand in uproarious laughter.

Why not take tango lessons? I remember what my father had to do to deck the train. "Screw your courage to the sticking place, then take a leap."

Katie Nolan

Author's Notes

General Notes

In chapter one, I believe the seeders my father and I used were Cahoon's Broadcast Seeders. They were popular in the 1940s and claimed to sow from four to eight acres in an hour at normal walking pace. It had a side mounted hand crank and was patented in the USA in 1861 www.antiquefarmtools. info/page3.htm. I calculated that my father must have worked a twelve hour day before I got there in the afternoon to help him finish seeding the field.

In chapter twelve, Union Square March, March 6 of 1930, see pp. 184 to 187 in *Pages from a Workers Life* by William Z. Foster to get an historical account. To quote Foster, The unemployed came together "to demand the right to live." In my book, I quote William Z. Foster with "Shall we march in spite of Whalen and his police?" Other than that, I imagined Foster's speech and some of the other details of the march, but I stayed true to history, in that each detail is based upon what actually happened.

In chapter twelve, I refer to the Everett Massacre, reminded of it when I pass through Everett on the train. I found this description of the massacre from *Hard Traveling, A Portrait of Work Life in the New Northwest*, Carlos Arnaldo Schwantes, University of Nebraska Press, Lincoln, 1994, 234 pp. "Everett Memorial on May Day 1917. When the oppressive tactics of Everett employers clashed with IWW assertiveness, the result was tragedy. A free speech fight began when the Wobblies intervened in a strike...by shingle workers... In response, local deputies beat Wobblies and expelled them from town. Hoping to avoid the lawmen who patrolled the highways and rail lines into Everett, more than two hundred Wobblies sailed north from Seattle on the steamship Verona on November 5, 1916. A gun-toting force of deputies awaited them on the Everett dock. Shots rang out—from where was never

232

proven—and when the firing stopped moments later, five Wobblies and two deputies lay dying. Several panicked Wobblies jumped overboard and apparently drowned..." Courtesy Archives of Labor and Urban Affairs, Wayne State University. From *Hard Traveling*, p. 63.

In chapter fifteen, Bud's sidekick Harry mentions anarcho-syndicalism. There are many definitions of anarcho-sydicalism, but I like this one
from Wikipedia:
"Anarcho-syndicalism (also referred to as revolutionary socialism) is a theory of anarchism which views revolutionary industrial unionism or syndicalism as a method of workers in capitalist society to gain control of an economy and, with that control, influence broader society." My understanding of anarcho-syndicalism is that workers could gain control of the economy through unions, thus, become the owners of the various businesses for which they presently work.

In chapter fifteen, and others, the IWW is mentioned because Bud's sidekick Harry is an organizer for the IWW. I found this definition in Wikipedia:
"The Industrial Workers of the world (IWW), members of which are commonly termed the Wobblies, is an international labor union that was founded in 1905 in Chicago, Illinois in the United States of America. The union combines general unionism with industrial unionism, as it is a general union whose members are further organized within the industry of their employment. The philosophy and tactics of the IWW are described as "revolutionary industrial unionism", with ties to both socialist and anarchist labor movements....The IWW promotes the concept of "One Big Union," and contends that all workers should be united as a social class to supplant capitalism and wage labor..." In 2012, the IWW moved its General Headquarters offices to 2036 West Montrose, Chicago."

One thing that is remarkable, for me, about the IWW is that it was quite before its time, welcoming women, immigrants, African Americans, and Asian Americans into their movement. In fact, there were many famous women leaders in the IWW, including Elizabeth Gurley Finn, Lucy Parsons, Mary Harris "Mother" Jones, and others.

In chapter 21, the story of the rescue of the man from Turkey Creek logging camp is loosely based upon William Z. Foster's description of the working conditions in the camp, and the rest was imagined based upon stories my father had told. William Z. Foster, *Pages From a Workers Life*, "Peonage in Florida," pp. 23-26.

In chapter 27, I allude to the Great Recession in the context of the loss of my home through foreclosure. I was curious about the official dates for this recession and looked it up. "The National Bureau of Economic Research (NBER) dates the beginning of the recession as December 2007. According to the Department of Labor, roughly 8.7 million jobs were shed from February 2008 to February 2010, and GDP contracted by 5.1%, making the Great Recession the worst since the Great Depression." From Wikipedia.

Notes on Anarchism

The entire book calls for a definition of anarchism, because my father's stance in the world, although not always coherent, often matched much of the theory of anarchism. Of course, in my courses on philosophy, I also studied anarchism, and after a long stint of embracing democratic socialism, came around to agreeing with the type of anarchism described by Noam Chomsky and David Graeber. I also voted for Bernie Sanders, a socialist, in our last election, and would do so again in a minute, so I suppose my anarchism would not be considered pure by all theorists.

Noam Chomsky's argument explaining why men and women are not free and equal in a representative democracy, was one of the turning points in my thinking on political theory: "Representative democracy, as in, say, the United States or Great Britain, would be criticized by an anarchist of this school on two grounds. First of all because there is a monopoly of power centralized in the state, and secondly—and critically—because the representative democracy is limited to the political sphere and in no serious way encroaches on the economic sphere. Anarchists of this tradition have always held that democratic control of one's productive life is at the core of any serious human liberation, or, for that matter, of any significant democratic practice. That is, as long as individuals are compelled to rent themselves on the market to those who are willing to hire them, as long as their role in production is simply that of ancillary tools, then there are striking elements of coercion and oppression that make talk of democracy very limited, if even meaningful." From an interview by Peter Jay..., July 25, 1976.

Noam Chomsky makes clear, in another part of this interview, that this type of socialism [anarcho-sydicalism] is voluntary. For me that means that there would be no compulsion to participate in anarcho-syndicalism, or any other type of anarchism or socialism, that the individual would freely decide whether they wished to do so. This, of course, eliminates one of the most egregious aspects of earlier forms of socialism/communism that were instituted by the Soviet Union, China, etc.

This definition of anarchism is by Alexander Berkman:
   "Anarchism means that you should be free; that no one should enslave you, boss you, rob you, or impose upon you.
   It means that you should be free to do the things that you want to do; and that you should not be compelled to do what you don't want to do. It means that you should have a chance to choose the kind of life you want to live, and live it without anybody interfering.
   It means that the next fellow should have the same freedom as you, that everyone should have the same rights and liberties.
   It means that all men are brothers, and that they should live like brothers, in peace and harmony. That is to say, that there should be no war, no violence used by one set of men against another, no monopoly and no poverty, no oppression, no taking advantage of your fellow man.
   In short, Anarchism means a condition or society where all men and women are free, and where all enjoy equally the benefits of an ordered and sensible life." Berkman, Alexander, *What is Anarchism*, AK Press, Oakland, 2003.

Books

For more information about anarchism, hobos, and the Great Depression, I found these books helpful:

Berkman, Alexander, *What is Anarchism?* AK Press, Edinburgh, London, Oakland, 2003, 237 pp. (This is a classic work on anarchism and it is written in "plain and simple language." In the Introduction, Berkman says, "I want to tell you about it in such plain and simple language that there will be no misunderstanding it."

Boxcar Bertha, an Autobiography, as told to Dr. Ben Reitman, Amok Press, New York, 1988, 285 pp.

Conover, Ted, *Rolling Nowhere*, Vintage Books, A Division of Random House, Inc., New York, 281 pp.

Depastino, Todd, *Citizen Hobo*, The University of Chicago Press, Chicago, 2003, 325 pp.

Foster, William Z., *Pages from a Workers Life*, International Publishers, New York, 1939. (The Turkey Creek rescue in chapter 21 was inspired by Foster's actual rescue of the peonage camp worker.)

Goodman, Edward C., ed., *Writing the Rails*, Black Dog and Leventhal Publishers, New York, 2001, 368 pp. (Especially the article by Dale Wasserman on pp. 170-179, "Flipping the Meat Train".)

Graeber, David, *Fragments of an Anarchist Anthropology, Prickly Paradigm* Press LLC, Chicago, 2004. (This was a pamphlet, later made into a paperback book. This book was also a turning point, for me, from a socialist perspective to an anarchist perspective.)

Holm, Monte and Dennis L. Clay, *Once a Hobo... The Autobiography of Monte Holm*, Proctor Publications, LLC, Ann Arbor, Michigan, 1999, 310 pp. (Although I use Monte as one of my father's sidekicks, this Monte is not related in any way, except for the inspiration gotten that the friend was going to found a junk shop enterprise. I was given the book by the secretary of my philosophy department, who discussed the fact with me that her uncle had been a hobo, then, produced this book and told me I could have it. I found it to be a treasure and it has made me wonder how many people in my generation have had relatives that rode the rails to find work).

Lasher, M. H., *Logging Chance*, The John C. Winston Company, 1944, 261 pp. (I was charmed when I found this book in a used bookstore in Port Townsend, WA. It has beautiful drawings by Hamilton Greene, and on the inside cover it says "Pocket Book, Jrs. are exciting, gay, worthwhile books for modern teen-agers. To get the best in reading always look for this trademark." Much detail in this book matches what my father told me about logging camps, choker-setters, etc. Even though this book was published long after the Great Depression, it demonstrates that workers were still struggling with difficult and dangerous working conditions.

Schwantes, Carlos Arnaldo, *Hard Traveling, A Portrait of Work Life in the New Northwest*, University of Nebraska Press, Lincoln, 1994, 234 pp.

Anarchism:

The name given to a principle or theory of life and conduct under which society is conceived without government—harmony in such a society being obtained, not by submission to law, or by obedience to any authority, but by free agreements concluded between the various groups, territorial and professional, freely constituted for the sake of production and consumption, as also for the satisfaction of the infinite variety of needs and aspirations of a civilized being.
Peter Kropotkin (Encyclopedia Brittanica)

Katie Nolan

Acknowledgements

It is no exaggeration to say that this book would not exist without my dear, decades-long friend, Deborah Woodard. I am often overwhelmed by her generosity and loyalty. She not only slogged through multiple early drafts, Deborah also gave me moral support and wise and insightful advice. I wish to thank Lana Hechtman Ayers, my mentor and treasured friend, who gave me the suggestions I needed to take this book to the next level. I can never express enough gratitude to Deborah and Lana for all they have done for me. I am also indebted to my amazing friend-in-the-spirit, Sharron Severson, for reading the manuscript and giving me great advice and loving support.
A special thank you to my writing teacher at Hugo House, Dickey Nesenger, who early on encouraged me to get my characters on the train.
Such a wonderful and insightful teacher!

I hope all of you aforementioned women know how important you are to me!

I also wish to thank Hedgebrook for making me believe I was a writer, Hypatia-in-the-Woods, and their wonderfully kind board of directors, for giving me the time and space for writing the final draft, and Centrum Port Townsend Writers' Conference, for the scholarships that allowed me to take workshops from such amazing writers as Dorothy Allison and Pam Houston. And thank you to the wonderful technical staff at Jefferson County Library, Chris, Daniel, Russ and all the rest! You are generous with your time and you are format wizards!

238

Made in the USA
Columbia, SC
02 August 2019